M366 Block 5
UNDERGRADUATE COMPUTING

Natural and artificial intelligence

Evolutionary computation

Block

5

Cover image: Daniel H. Janzen. *Polistes* wasps build a relatively simple nest that lasts only a single summer. These New World wasps often site the unenclosed combs under eaves and the other sheltered places where they come into contact with people.

This publication forms part of an Open University course M366 *Natural and artificial intelligence*. Details of this and other Open University courses can be obtained from the Student Registration and Enquiry Service, The Open University, PO Box 197, Milton Keynes MK7 6BJ, United Kingdom: tel. +44 (0)845 300 6090, email general-enquiries@open.ac.uk

Alternatively, you may visit the Open University website at http://www.open.ac.uk where you can learn more about the wide range of courses and packs offered at all levels by The Open University.

To purchase a selection of Open University course materials visit http://www.ouw.co.uk, or contact Open University Worldwide, Michael Young Building, Walton Hall, Milton Keynes MK7 6AA, United Kingdom for a brochure. tel. +44 (0)1908 858785; fax +44 (0)1908 858787; email ouwenq@open.ac.uk

The Open University
Walton Hall, Milton Keynes
MK7 6AA

First published 2007, Second edition 2008.

Edited and designed by The Open University.

Typeset by SR Nova Pvt. Ltd, Bangalore, India.

Printed and bound in the United Kingdom by The Charlesworth Group, Wakefield.

ISBN 978 0 7492 5096 6

2.1

Block 5
Evolutionary computing

Prepared for the course team by Mike Richards,
Neil Smith and Chris Dobbyn

CONTENTS

M366 COURSE TEAM

Chair, author and academic editor
Chris Dobbyn

Authors
Mustafa Ali

Tony Hirst

Mike Richards

Neil Smith

Patrick Wong

External assessor
Nigel Crook, Oxford Brookes University

Course managers
Gaynor Arrowsmith

Linda Landsberg

Media development staff
Andrew Seddon, Media Project Manager

Garry Hammond, Editor

Kate Gentles, Freelance Editor

Callum Lester, Software Developer

Andrew Whitehead, Designer and Graphic Artist

Phillip Howe, Compositor

Sarah Gamman, Contracts Executive

Lydia Eaton, Media Assistant

Critical readers
Frances Chetwynd

John Dyke

Ian Kenny

Paolo Remagnino

Thanks are due to the Desktop Publishing Unit of the Faculty of Mathematics and Computing.

Introduction to Block 5

Block introduction

> Time and favourable conditions are the two principal means which nature
> has employed in giving existence to all her productions. We know that for her
> time has no limit, and that consequently she always has it at her disposal.
>
> Source: Lamarck, J.-B. (1801)

Arching over all the theory, the detail and the mathematics, M366 has one clear
theme. It is this: in every age, scientific theory and technological discovery combine
to yield new understandings of humanity and our place in the world, and new ways
of tackling age-old problems. In particular, you have seen how, in the late twentieth
and early twenty-first centuries, *biological* theories and ever-increasing *computing*
power have united to bring about new approaches to the problems of artificial
intelligence (AI) and computational problem solving, along with new insights into the
nature of intelligence and problem solving themselves.

A long time ago, back in Block 1, I asked to you to identify some of the dominant
technologies of the twentieth century. At that point, I singled out the digital computer
for discussion, but of course many others must have suggested themselves. Throughout
history, war has always been – tragically – a crucible for new technologies. The
aftermath of the Second World War saw two significant discoveries that were to shape
the scientific and technological evolution of the second half of the twentieth century.
The first, the 1947 invention of the transistor by William Shockley, John Bardeen
and Walter Brattain at Bell Labs in New Jersey, made possible the semiconductor
revolution and modern computing technology.

In 1952, a second discovery spawned a revolution in molecular biology and the
biochemical sciences that is still reshaping our world. The identification of the structure
of *deoxyribonucleic acid* (DNA) was made by James Watson and Francis Crick in
Cambridge, inspired by the work of Rosalind Franklin and Maurice Wilkins of Kings
College, London. This discovery led to Nobel Prizes for Watson, Crick and Wilkins,
in 1962. Franklin died from cancer in 1958 and, as it is a tradition that the Nobel Prize
is not awarded posthumously, at the time her work did not achieve the same level
of recognition as that of her colleagues. It is only since the 1990s that she has been
given due recognition and her work has been commemorated in the Rosalind
Franklin Award of the Royal Society for outstanding contributions to natural science,
engineering or technology.

Block 5, the final main part of our course, tells the story of how Darwin's theory of
evolution by natural selection, the understanding that DNA offers of how hereditary
traits are transmitted from generation to generation, and the digital and silicon
technologies of the computer have come together in a whole new strategy for
computational problem solving: evolutionary computation.

Unit 1: Unleashing the gene genie: an introduction to evolutionary algorithms

In Unit 1, I will review some of the biological theory underlying evolutionary computation,
including a recap of the theory of natural selection and a brief discussion of our modern
understanding of heredity and its mechanisms, which centres on that amazing
molecule, *deoxyribonucleic acid* (DNA). I then introduce the idea of a *genetic algorithm*
(GA), a very simplified model of the processes of evolution and inheritance. My
discussion will cover the basic building blocks of GAs and is based on a number
of worked examples and case studies that demonstrate how GAs can be applied
to optimisation problems.

Unit 2: Genetic algorithms

In Unit 2, I examine some of the theory of evolutionary computation, including schema theory, Markov processes and the intriguingly named 'No-Free-Lunch' theorem.

Unit 3: Artificial evolution

Finally, Unit 3 considers two other areas in which evolutionary computing can be applied. The first of these is in *genetic programming* (GP), in which computer programs themselves can be evolved. The discussion includes a short case study illustrating a practical application of genetic programming. The second area I consider is *evolutionary robotics*, where the same evolutionary principles that are found in GAs and GP are used to develop controllers for reactive robots – generally some form of neural network. This discussion will take us into advanced theoretical questions in artificial evolution, such as co-evolution, the interaction between evolution and learning, and the mapping between genotype and phenotype.

Block 5 learning outcomes

After studying this block you will be able to:

▶ write an outline explanation of the biological foundations of evolutionary computation (EC), illustrating the concepts of chromosomes, genes, recombination, mutation and selection under Darwinian evolution;

▶ write a concise account, with diagrams, of the principal elements of a genetic algorithm (GA): strings, populations, biased roulette wheels, etc.;

▶ write a set of bullets explaining the processes associated with the above elements as the GA runs forward in time;

▶ explain, with examples, some of the statistical principles that are operating as string populations evolve over time in a GA system;

▶ list, with examples, the components of a genetic programming (GP) system;

▶ write a description of one robotic system in which GA techniques have been used;

▶ write a short reflective essay describing the relationship between biological systems and EC systems; the shortcomings and strengths of EC; and the implications of an understanding of EC to the wider problems of AI and computerised problem solving.

Unit 1: Unleashing the gene genie: an introduction to evolutionary algorithms

CONTENTS

Introduction to Unit 1

As you've just read in the introduction to this block, and in the learning outcomes I have defined for it, the theme of this final major part of the course is **evolutionary computing**. This family of computational intelligence techniques is inspired by our scientific understanding of biological evolution and inheritance. However, we shall also see how evolutionary computation gains inspiration from everyday, common-sense models of evolution and the mechanisms of inheritance.

Evolutionary computing (EC) or *evolutionary algorithms* (EAs) are general terms I will use to cover a range of computational techniques going under such names as *genetic algorithms* (GAs), *genetic programming* (GP), *evolutionary programming* (EP) and *evolution strategies* (ES). You will meet some of these in detail later in the block. But although there are many different styles of evolutionary algorithm (and perhaps many more yet to be invented), they are all based on the same abstract model of a general evolutionary system. In this model, all of the four mechanisms that have dominated our thinking since Block 3 – *interaction*, *emergence*, *adaptation* and *selection* – come together.

Here is the ground plan of this unit. In the first section I will quickly review the basic concepts of Darwinian evolution, which you met in Unit 2 of Block 3. As you may recall, Darwin's theory depends on the idea of advantageous characteristics of an organism being inherited reliably by its offspring. A serious problem for the theory – one that Darwin himself recognised – was that there was at that time no real explanation of how inheritance worked. Section 2 deals with our modern understanding of heredity and its mechanisms, which is based entirely on that remarkable molecule *deoxyribonucleic acid* (DNA).

But our purpose in M366 has been all along to show how biological theory can be linked to computing power to solve age-old problems in new ways. Section 3 introduces the idea of a *genetic algorithm*, a model (as always, a highly simplified one) of the processes of evolution and inheritance. Here I will introduce the basic building blocks of a GA and show how these can be manipulated to produce solutions to difficult problems – in particular, our old friend the *optimisation problem*.

Section 4 looks forward to some of the variations on the basic theme of the GA that I will talk about later in the block. Finally, Section 5 presents some examples of problems in strategy and optimisation that GAs have been successfully used for.

What you need to study this unit

You will need the following course components, and will need to use your computer and internet connection for some of the exercises.

▶ this Block 5 text
▶ the course DVD.

LEARNING OUTCOMES FOR UNIT 1

After studying this unit you will be able to:

1.1 write a set of bullet points outlining and contrasting the main principles of Lamarckian and Darwinian evolution;

1.2 write a short paragraph outlining the biological basis of inheritance, in terms of chromosomes, genes and meiosis;

1.3 draw a diagram illustrating the structure of the DNA molecule, illustrating and labelling the base pairs;

1.4 write short definitions of the following terms as they relate to GAs: *genome*, *gene*, *population*, *mutation*, *crossover*, *fitness function*, *fitness landscape*;

1.5 give an example of the manner in which a problem solution can be represented by an artificial genome;

1.6 explain the main steps of a GA using a detailed worked example;

1.7 write a set of bullet points explaining some suggested improvements to the basic GA structure;

1.8 write a short paragraph relating biological theory to the steps of a GA;

1.9 describe a number of potential applications for GAs.

2 Evolution

For all the controversy, bitterness, soul-searching and even violence that the concept of evolution has caused, and continues to cause to this day, the idea is hardly a new one. The ancient Greeks had no word for 'evolution', but the pre-Socratic philosopher Anaximander (610–564 BCE) noted that all living organisms developed gradually and suggested that humans may have originated from animals of other species – possibly aquatic ones. Aristotle (384–322 BCE) saw nature as imbued with a kind of evolutionary purpose. The lowest organisms were formed from primeval matter by a gradual process of transition, he believed; and he envisaged a continuous progression from simple, undeveloped forms to the higher and more perfect ones. Outside Europe, it has been suggested that the Indian sage Patañjali (possibly born 2nd century BCE) entertained evolutionary ideas.

However, modern belief in evolution only started to harden after the European Enlightenment, as ideas of social and cultural progress began to be applied to the natural world. There is no space here for an account of this: it's sufficient to point to two outstanding figures – the Frenchman Jean-Baptiste Lamarck (1744–1829) and the Englishman Charles Darwin (1809–1882).

2.1 Lamarckian evolution

Lamarck formulated the first truly modern theory of evolution in 1801. He proposed that organisms were moulded by their environment and passed these changes on to their descendants. For instance, a blacksmith would acquire a muscular physique after a lifetime's work at the forge. According to Lamarck's theory, he would then pass his increased muscularity on to his children; and so, over many generations, the descendants of the blacksmith would become increasingly muscular (so long as they remained in manual professions). Lamarckism was eventually discredited by the work of Mendel. However, as the quotation at the beginning of this block suggests, credit must be given to him for realising that great changes can happen to living organisms, given sufficient time, and that the evolution of species was governed by processes that could be explained by science.

2.2 Darwinian evolution

Whilst Darwin is generally credited with the theory of natural selection, a fellow biologist, Alfred Russell Wallace, had independently come to the same conclusion. A warning that Russell was about to announce his theory forced Darwin to publish *On the Origin of Species* in 1859. Some textbooks now jointly credit Darwin and Wallace with the discovery.

For a theory that has engendered so much controversy in the last 150 years, Charles Darwin's theory of evolution is surprisingly simple and elegant. I outlined the main ideas of Darwinian evolution in Unit 2 of Block 3. Let's review them briefly now.

SAQ 1.1

Outline in a set of bullet points the main points of Darwin's theory of evolution by natural selection.

ANSWER...

In Unit 2 of Block 3 I presented Darwin's chain of reasoning as follows:

1   Organisms produce more offspring than the environment could possibly support.

2   Members of a species struggle among themselves, and with other species, for the limited resources available in their environment.

3   Organisms vary.

4   Variants that are best equipped for the struggle survive long enough to reproduce and pass on their advantageous features to the next generation, while less well-adapted variants die before they can reproduce.

5   Thus, species gradually adapt to their environmental conditions.

Darwin's ideas were forged in the remote Galapagos Islands of the Pacific. There, he observed new species of animals previously unknown to science. However, these isolated animals were similar to those found across South America and so, Darwin reasoned, might have originated across the ocean. Similar, but not identical – the species on the Galapagos showed adaptations to the unique climate and terrain of the islands. Most tellingly, Darwin observed how the beaks of the species of finches on each island were exquisitely specialised to cope with the vegetation of that island alone. He was also aware, as were most educated men of his age, that the fossil record appeared to show that the complexity of life on Earth has been increasing with time, from smears of carbon found in the very earliest rocks – believed to be fossils of microscopic single-celled organisms – to the immense variety of species we see on the modern planet. The radiation of species led some early evolutionists to theorise that evolution was *directed* towards the production and perfection of advanced organisms, with humanity at its very apex.

There are three vital points I want to make at this stage, and which must be borne in mind in any discussion of evolution.

▶   Evolutionary mechanisms are entirely blind. There is no need for a guiding intelligence. The idea that order can appear without some controller or plan always seems counterintuitive to purposeful creatures like us. We do not expect to pour a collection of building blocks onto the floor and find them fall into the shape of a model house. But evolution *can* produce order; organisms are exposed to a never-ending series of environmental tests which they must overcome using the characteristics they have inherited from their ancestors. Individuals that lack a characteristic, or do not have it to the highest degree, are penalised by death, or at best failure to breed. After many successive generations, the numbers of organisms equipped with the best characteristics will grow, whilst less well-equipped individuals will become increasingly rare and eventually disappear altogether. The idea that order can arise from random processes has been a consistent theme of M366.

▶   Because evolutionary mechanisms are blind, there is no *goal* to evolution. Nor is there any *moral* dimension to natural selection. The Victorian idea that evolution had produced some kind of hierarchy, at the summit of which stood humanity, is quite wrong. An even more poisonous falsehood is the concept of 'social Darwinism' – the convenient myth that those at the top of the social hierarchy, the wealthy and the powerful, have succeeded in the struggle for existence as a result of special merit: that they are, in some sense, morally fitter and more deserving than the rest.

The oldest known rocks on Earth are more than 3.8 billion years old. Analysis of their carbon content suggests that single-celled life was present at this time. Billions of years passed before these organisms evolved into anything more complex. It was once thought that multi-cellular life might have originated 'only' 580 million years ago. However, fossilised worm casts found in India have been dated to 1.1 billion years ago. Nevertheless, it is worth remembering that for almost three-quarters of the Earth's history, the only life forms were microscopic.

▶ A crucial point in the Darwinian argument presented above, in the answer to SAQ 1.1, was step 3: *organisms vary*. But what kind of variation are we talking about here? In Unit 2 of Block 3 I distinguished between adaptations that take place over the lifetime of the individual and adaptation over many generations. The simple fact is that Lamarck was wrong: most adaptations that take place over an individual's lifespan cannot be passed on to that individual's offspring. The fact that I've taken to working out in the gym recently, and have become rather less feeble than I once was, does not mean that any children I may have will be muscular. Only certain *heritable* variations can be passed on. I will discuss the nature of these shortly.

Let's sum this all up in the following question.

SAQ 1.2

Briefly describe the differences between Lamarckian and Darwinian evolution.

ANSWER...

Whilst at first glance Darwinian evolution and Lamarckian evolution may seem to be quite similar, there are significant differences. Lamarck saw individual creatures as plastic; they were shaped by their environment with the results being passed to future generations. Darwin proposed that individuals were tested by their environment. Those that possessed some form of advantageous characteristics were most likely to thrive, breed and pass these advantages on to future generations.

Darwin's theory depends on the proposition that every living individual possesses a set of unique inheritable characteristics – larger leaves, a thicker coat of fur, greater intelligence, and so on. The environment constantly tests these characteristics: a furry creature would survive better in colder climates than those with less fur, and would live to pass on its furry coat to its descendants. But scientists of the time were entirely ignorant as to *how* such characteristics were transmitted to future generations. Darwin had no proper theory of inheritance at his command.

Darwin's contemporaries presented this as a major stumbling block to acceptance of his theory. But in reality, this isn't so. From time immemorial it has been known that characteristics are passed from parents to children. Almost all of us will have commented on a child having 'his mother's eyes' or 'her father's hair'. Physical characteristics run in families, such as the well-known protuberant 'Hapsburg lip', seen in portraits of many members of that European dynasty. And children resemble their parents not just in physical form, but also in their predisposition to certain diseases. The best-known example is the prevalence of haemophilia amongst European royal families. Queen Victoria appears to have been the originator of the condition, and it was spread through her children's marriages into other European royal families, as can be seen in Figure 1.1. Haemophilia was eventually diagnosed amongst Victoria's descendants in the British, Spanish, German and Russian courts.

So Darwin had proposed a theory of evolution that was supported by real-world evidence, but lacked a well-understood mechanism that would explain the heritability of characteristics on which the whole theory depended. Despite his attempts to promote his own pangenetic theory of heredity, it was only the later work of Mendel and the development of genetic theory that placed evolution on a firm founding. I'll offer an outline of this work now.

Tsarevich Alexei Nikolaevich of Russia's haemophilia had grave consequences. Alexei's mother came under the influence of the monk Grigori Rasputin, who claimed that he could cure the child. His relationship with the Tsarina caused popular outrage, culminating in the February Revolution of 1917 and the abdication of the Russian royal family. By November 1917, Russia had become the world's first communist dictatorship.

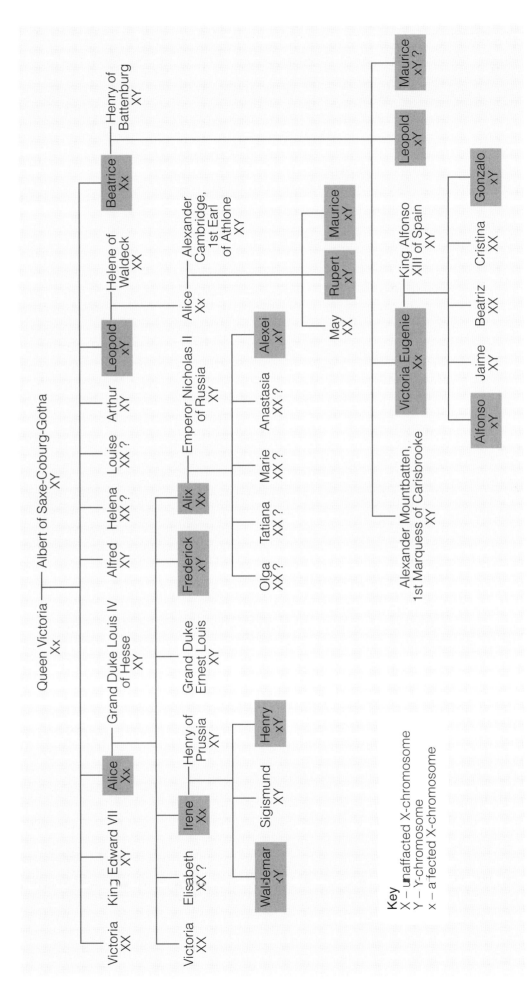

Figure 1.1   The British haemophilia line

3 Inheritance as a biological process

Attempts to explain the process of inheritance scientifically had been made since the time of Aristotle, but it was Darwin – recognising a need for such a theory – who proposed the first serious modern account of hereditary mechanisms.

3.1 Darwin and Mendel

According to Darwin's pangenetic account of inheritance, every part of an animal's body produced a discrete 'seed', which he called a *gemmule*, capable of forming a similar part in the child; the full set of gemmules was gathered inside the reproductive organs and passed on during reproduction. The theory never attracted much support, chiefly because gemmules themselves proved elusive. Instead, many biologists preferred the pangenetic theory of the Dutch biologist Hugo de Vries. De Vries had conducted experiments in which he hybridised varieties of evening primrose, and came to the conclusion that the plants contained discrete 'particles' of inheritance, which he termed *pangenes*, that were passed from parents to their children. But de Vries knew that he was not the first person to come to this conclusion. As early as the 1890s, he had discovered an obscure 1865 scientific paper by a Czech monk, Gregor Mendel, but failed to mention this earlier research in the reports of his experiments he published in 1900. De Vries corrected what I will charitably call an 'oversight' after criticism by the German biologist Carl Correns, who had independently rediscovered Mendel's work on inheritance.

In 1875, Oscar Hertwig, a German biologist, was the first to observe the microscopic process of reproduction by which an egg is penetrated by a sperm. Hertwig may only have been studying sea urchins, but his discovery proved that sexual reproduction involved the transfer of some form of material responsible for inheritance.

3.2 Chromosomes

The late nineteenth century saw huge improvements in the field of microscopy. Not only did far greater levels of magnification become available, but new techniques of staining specimens with indelible dyes made it possible to resolve structures inside living cells. Biologists' attention turned to a small dark blob of material lying deep within the interior of most cells, known as the **nucleus**.

The X and Y chromosomes determine sex in humans, but other species use other chromosomes: ducks have two completely different sex chromosomes, Z and W; whilst the duck-billed platypus has ten sex chromosomes! What it does with them all is still a mystery.

When cells were stained, certain parts of the nucleus took up more dye than others, in particular certain strand-like structures that became known as **chromosomes** (see Figure 1.2). The number of chromosomes was found to vary between species: whilst mice manage with just twenty, humans possess forty-six. The number of chromosomes in an organism seems to have little or nothing to do with intelligence or complexity: both chimpanzees and tobacco plants possess forty-eight chromosomes. Most chromosomes come in pairs: the first forty-four human chromosomes form twenty-two neat pairs. However, the remaining two may or may not form a pair: women have a pair of X-shaped structures; men possess one large X-shaped chromosome, and one tiny Y-shaped chromosome.

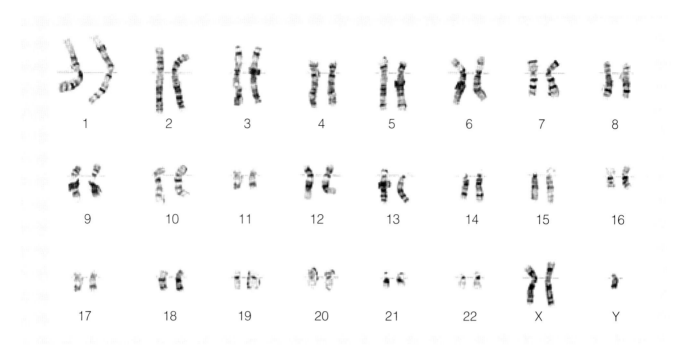

Figure 1.2 Human chromosomes. This diagram (known as a karyotype) shows pairs of chromosomes lined up in order from the largest (chromosome 1) to the shortest (chromosome 22). The two sex chromosomes are shown at the bottom-right. This karyotype contains an X chromosome and a Y chromosome and has therefore been taken from a man. A woman's karyotype would contain two X chromosomes

Biologists quickly concluded that chromosomes were responsible for carrying inheritance information. Each pair of chromosomes consisted of one contributed by the mother and one from the father. The final pair of chromosomes – either XX or XY – related to the sex of the child, the X chromosome could come from either parent, but the Y chromosome only from the father.

3.3 Inside the chromosome – genes

Mendel's theory required that inheritance information was made up from individual grains, named **genes**, each responsible for some fundamental characteristic of an organism, such as the colour of its hair and eyes, its height, and so on. The chromosome seemed a plausible location for these genes, a hypothesis proven by the work of Thomas Hunt Morgan and his student Alfred H. Sturtevant. From 1910 onwards, the pair had studied the genetics of the fruit fly *Drosophila*. They not only demonstrated how successive generations of fruit flies inherited characteristics from their parents, but were also able to start mapping the location of specific genes on the flies' chromosomes.

The word 'gene' was coined as late as 1909 by the Danish botanist Wilhelm Johanssen. William Bateson first used the term 'genetics' in 1905.

What was missing from the explanation of inheritance was *how* genes created new organisms. In 1902 Archibald Garrod had proposed that each gene was responsible for the manufacture of a single protein in an organism, a hypothesis that was not proven until 1942. But as so often in science, this answer only raised further questions – *what* were genes; what were they *made from*? Analyses conducted during the 1920s and 1930s suggested that they were composed of proteins, a theory disproved in 1944 when attention turned to a shadowy molecule lurking amongst the proteins – **deoxyribonucleic acid** (**DNA**).

It is now known that this is a simplification; while in many cases one gene does manufacture a single protein, other genes control the action of further genes.

DNA is slippery stuff, literally and figuratively. Isolated in the test tube, it resembles unbeaten egg white – a colourless or slightly milky, slimy substance offering no outward sign of its being the most powerful molecule in the world. This undistinguished-looking chemical was discovered in 1869, but for the first half of the twentieth century, biologists assumed that it was an inconsequential molecule, possibly acting as scaffolding for the proteins that carried inheritance information in the gene. In fact, the opposite is true. We now recognise chromosomes as compact spools of DNA tightly wound around protein molecules.

DNA is what is known as a **polymer**, a molecule made up from smaller building blocks, in this case composed of units known as *nucleotides*. Each nucleotide is in turn made from a simple sugar molecule, a phosphate and one of four amino acid *bases* – adenine (**A**), cytosine (**C**), guanine (**G**) and thymine (**T**). Each base has a distinctive molecular shape that makes it possible for it to be weakly linked to other bases in pairs. **A** will link only to **T** (and therefore **T** links only to **A**), whilst **C** will link only to **G** (and thus **G** only to **C**). A single molecule of DNA contains unimaginably large numbers of these pairs of bases, stacked in a spiral pattern – the famous double-helix discovered by Crick and Watson (see Figure 1.3).

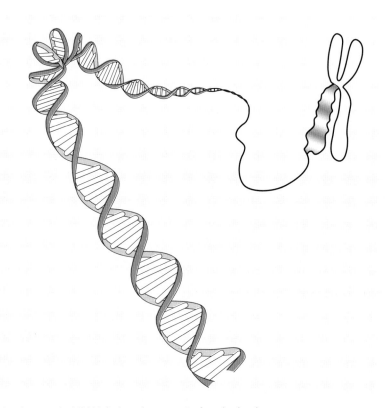

Figure 1.3   A strand of DNA being drawn out of a single chromosome

Early researchers believed that the bases in DNA would be a monotonous repetition like those of other polymers, with endless repeating patterns such as **AT,GC,AT,GC,AT, GC,AT** ... etc. (Figure 1.4). But when they began to read the actual order of the base pairs, they found that the bases appeared to show little or no repetition – a sequence might read **AT,CG,GC,TA,TA,GC,AT,GC,AT,CG,AT,AT,GC** ... or there might be hundreds of **AT** pairs one after another.

We now know that DNA is a kind of digital data store. The arrangement of bases along a piece of DNA is somewhat akin to a computer program, and is a recipe for manufacturing proteins inside a cell. The whole of an organism's inheritance information held in its DNA is known as its **genome**. In the case of a virus this might only amount to a few thousand bases; for humans, more than three billion. The human genome comprises some 30 000 genes, but these form only 2% of all the DNA found in our cells.

The remainder is apparently inert and goes by the name **junk DNA**, or, more politely, **non-coding DNA**. This extra DNA partly explains the disparities in the sizes of the genomes of various organisms. The size of the genome does not increase with increasing complexity; genomes are far more variable than that. For instance, the genome of a human being is only one-twentieth the size of that of an onion and less than 0.5% the size of the genome of a single-celled amoeba. Yet, with only a few exceptions, humans are more interesting and intelligent than either the onion or the amoeba. The origin of non-coding DNA, and its purpose, if any, remain unknown.

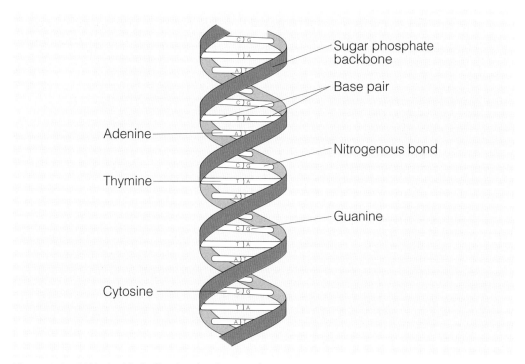

Figure 1.4   DNA double helix showing base pairs

The DNA in a single cell might exist for a few days or weeks, or for decades, but none of it will survive the death of its host. However, the *information* contained in these strands can continue to exist as long as there are offspring to inherit it. Inheritance is the result of these intricate patterns of bases, encoded in genes, passing from generation to generation. Left unaltered, the same sequence of bases will produce identical characteristics over hundreds, even millions of generations. It is truly remarkable that DNA remains largely unchanged over millions of years. Humans not only bear a striking resemblance to the great apes, we also share a great deal of genetic information – over 99% in the case of chimpanzees. So, it is only that 1% of our genes that makes the difference between one species performing in tea bag advertisements and the other species watching them. Much of our genome is incredibly ancient: approximately 75% of our DNA can also be found in nematodes – tiny, soil-dwelling worms – and we share approximately half of our genes with the humble banana. Biologists increasingly use **phylogenetic analysis** – differences between the gonomoc of different species – to determine their relationships to one another. This has produced surprises. For example, zoologists once classified hippopotamuses as close relatives of pigs, on the grounds of their similar anatomies. However, analysis has shown that they are only distant relatives, pigs and hippos diverging long before hippos diverged from another group of mammals – the whales.

The tale of DNA, its workings within the cell and its role in the immensely complex molecular interactions involved in constructing the organism in which it resides, is a fascinating one, but not one that I can pursue any further here. Every day, biochemists discover new surprises and complexities. However, it is now time to return to the main theme of M366. How can we use these biological insights in working computer systems?

4 Genetic algorithms

The technologies of solid-state electronics and digital computing, and the science of the gene, have matured alongside one another. Advances in computing have powered the genetic revolution: supercomputers have made it possible to determine the exact genetic structures of many living organisms, including ourselves. They have helped build our understanding of these structures; they have even enabled us to 'rewind' the process of evolution by unravelling how one species is related to another.

However, biology has also inspired computer scientists, as you've seen throughout this course. And theories of biological evolution have had a direct influence on computing, in the invention of the **genetic algorithm** (GA). In Unit 1 of Block 3, I presented the struggle of an organism or a species to survive as a kind of problem-solving activity. Living creatures are perpetually faced with the 'trials of life'. One approach to surviving these trials is to evolve (over many generations) the body shapes, reaction times, protective devices and sensory systems that best suit the habitat a species inhabits. So, just as living organisms attempt to 'solve' the problem of staying alive and reproducing in a changing world by evolving, GAs *evolve* solutions to the problems set by their designers. Typical problems include determining the roots of a mathematical equation, determining the quickest route between several cities or simulating the behaviour of simple living creatures.

Remember, there is no conscious intention implied here. Organisms do not *decide* to evolve. Evolution has no plan.

4.1 GAs – the components

GAs are well suited to those problems characterised by a large search space in which some answers are more correct than others: combinatorial optimisation problems, for instance – in fact, many of the problems of AI. To take a very simple example, there is a range of answers to the question 'When was DNA discovered?' A precise answer could be '1869', but other more-or-less correct answers include 'the 1860s', 'the nineteenth century' and 'the second millennium AD'. Each answer is correct, although some answers are more correct (i.e. more useful) than others. We might arrange our answers in order of decreasing correctness as shown in Table 1.

Table 1.1

When was DNA discovered?	
1869	Most correct
The 1860s	
The nineteenth century	
The second millennium AD	Least correct

Let's now introduce the first of the elements of a GA, the idea of a **fitness landscape**.

Fitness landscape

You should be quite familiar by now with the idea of a *landscape*. You met the concept in Block 2, in connection with search; in our discussions of particle swarm optimisation (PSO) in Unit 3 of Block 3; and in the form of energy landscapes in

Unit 4 of Block 4. Now, once again, the search space of our little problem can be visualised as an undulating landscape; in this case the answer '1869' would sit very close to the peak of the highest hill. Close by, but slightly lower, would be the answers '1868' and '1870' – which are very nearly correct. 'The 1860s' would lie a little lower still down the hill; 'the nineteenth century' would be even lower, whilst 'the second millennium AD' would be found close to the foot of the hill.

Hill-climbing search, introduced in Block 2, Unit 2, is one strategy for tackling this type of problem. A GA is another. In essence, a GA attempts to find a solution to the problem by running *many* searches in *parallel*, a strategy comparable in some ways to the ant colony optimisation (ACO) and other swarm techniques I discussed in Unit 3 of Block 3, but in this case importing new ideas of the gene – reproduction, inheritance, fitness and natural selection – from evolutionary biology. With a GA we associate the peaks and troughs of the landscape with *fitness*. The highest hills represent the most fit points of the landscape, on the analogy of the organisms that are best adapted to their environment, the lowest hills, the least fit. We then try to *evolve* solutions to the problem.

Let's see how this works. In our fitness landscape, a GA does not use a single searcher, but many, perhaps many thousands, initially located randomly across the landscape. Each searcher is tested as a potential solution to the problem: those lying at points lower down the landscape (the less fit, the poorer solutions) are classified as failures and eliminated. Those lying close to fitness peaks survive to spawn new, nearby searchers. Some of these will lie even closer to the summit, others closer to the valleys. The test would be repeated for a second time, and then again. Over time, as the less fit searchers are progressively eliminated, and the fitter survive and reproduce, the population will converge on the highest peak, clustering around the best possible solution.

This might seem rather puzzling at the moment. I've been talking in the abstract about *searchers*; but what exactly are they? Here I take another inspiration from biology.

Genes, genomes and solutions

GAs use *artificial genes* strung along *genomes*. But instead of controlling the production of proteins, artificial genomes are strings storing ordered pieces of information – commonly these are strings of *bits* or binary values (**0** or **1**), often just referred to as **bit strings**. A bit might directly represent a Boolean value (true or false), or groups of bits can be strung together to store more complex values such as numbers. For example, we could create a genome to represent basic information about rooms, with just three genes – one for length, a second for width and a third representing the height. So, for a room 4 metres by 3 metres by 2 metres, we would have 4 (**100** in binary), then 3 (**011**), then 2 (**010**). Our genome would be **100011010**.

Genes are interpreted by external programs whose job is to evaluate these strings. To take a trivial example, consider a hypothetical genome that can be used to determine what to do with our spare time. The genome contains two genes, each one bit long. The first bit tells if it is daytime (in which case we will store a **1** in that gene) or night-time (i.e. not daytime) – in which case we will store a **0**. The second bit will store a **1** if it is a weekday, a **0** if it is the weekend (i.e. not a weekday). So the genome that stores daytime at a weekend is **10**, night-time during the week **01**, and so on.

A program can read this genome from left to right and choose the action to perform depending on the value of each gene. A computer program for reading our simple genome would look something like the one shown in Table 1.2.

Table 1.2

English description	Description in terms of genes

If it is **Daytime** then
    If it is a **Weekday** then
    Go to work
    Else if it is **Not** a **Weekday** then
    Go to the beach
Else if it is **Not Daytime** then
    If it is a **Weekday** then
    Watch TV
    Else if it is **Not** a **Weekday** then
    Go out to dinner
	If first gene is **1** then
	    If second gene is **1** then
	    Go to work
	    Else if second gene is **0** then
	    Go to the beach
	Else if first gene is **0** then
	    If second gene is **1** then
	    Watch TV
	    Else if second gene is **0** then
	    Go out to dinner

SAQ 1.3

Using the example genome above, what would the computer suggest we do if it was given the genome **10**?

ANSWER...

If we give the genome **10** to our computer, it will assess the value of the first bit (*Is it daytime?*) and conclude that it is daytime. The computer will then start executing the part of the program relevant to daytime. It examines the second bit (*Is it a weekday?*), containing a **0**, which determines that it is not a weekday – in which case our computer program tells us we should go to the beach – excellent advice!

As you can see, the sequence of zeros and ones has no *meaning* independent of the program that interprets it.

Since this idea of a genome is so important – indeed the foundation stone of GAs – let's try one further, rather more realistic, example. I will return for a moment to our sturdy companion the TSP. Once again, the details of our specimen five-city problem are given by Table 1.3.

Table 1.3

	Exeter	Bristol	Manchester	Leeds	London
Exeter	X	74	236	278	173
Bristol	74	X	165	207	119
Manchester	236	165	X	43	198
Leeds	278	207	43	X	195
London	173	119	198	195	X

Now consider this question.

Exercise 1.1

How would you represent a single tour of the five cities as a genome?

Discussion ....

For illustration, let's take the tour {Exeter, Manchester, London, Leeds, Bristol}. Genomes consist only of strings of bits, so first of all we need to represent each city by a unique string. As there are five cities, we will need three bits for each city (with some bits spare). I chose:

Exeter	000
Bristol	001
Manchester	010
Leeds	011
London	100

So the tour {Exeter, Manchester, London, Leeds, Bristol} is simply given by the string **000010100011001**.

Note that this doesn't tell us anything about whether the tour is any good or not (in fact, you can probably see it's an absolutely rotten one). The important point is that it represents a *potential solution* to the TSP when evaluated by a special program designed to estimate its fitness. Obviously such a program would place this tour at a very low position on our fitness landscape, so as a possible solution to the TSP it would not survive for long.

Programs that evaluate the fitness of a potential solution are essential to the working of any GA. They are known as **fitness functions**.

Fitness functions

Just as natural selection winnows out weaker genetic sequences, GAs test synthetic genomes, discarding the weaker strains. Unlike the amorphous, overlapping tests of survival found in the natural world, the tests faced by artificial genes are provided by clearly specified computer programs.

The tests used by GAs are known as *fitness functions*. The precise fitness function depends on the task. In the TSP, this is simply a matter of evaluating the length of the tour. In the case of another optimisation problem – protein folding, say – each genome would represent one possible folded configuration of the molecule, and the fitness function would measure the energy of that configuration.

See Block 1 Unit 1, for the example of protein folding as a problem in optimisation. See the course DVD for a discussion of the application of GAs to this problem.

The population

Most GAs start with a **population** of many genomes, with the genes of each member set to *random* values. The number of possible genomes is surprisingly large. For the tiny room genome in the previous section, each gene can take one of eight possible values, and since each genome contains three genes it can have one of 512 unique values ($8 \times 8 \times 8$, or, since the string is nine bits long, 2^9). Obviously, the number of possible genomes increases as the number of bits is increased. The TSP genome has fifteen bits, so there are $2^{15} = 32\,768$ possible genome values. (But not exactly that many *tours*: since we have some three-bit strings spare, which thus represent non-cities, there are fewer genuine tours.)

The precise number of genomes used in the program depends on factors such as the size of the search space (with larger problems needing more genes) and computer power (faster computers with more memory can handle more genomes). The number of genes in each genome depends on the problem being tackled.

Now, recall that the correct way to look at a genome in a GA is as *a potential solution to a problem*. Returning to the question of what to do with our time, we might articulate the problem as 'What are the conditions when I can go to the beach?'. In this case, only one arrangement of genes, **10**, represents the correct solution. We start with a number of random genomes – in this case that is not too demanding a task, there are only four possibilities – **00**, **01**, **10** and **11**. The computer can then evaluate the outcome of applying the tests above to each genome in turn; all except one will fail, only the genome **10** will tell us to 'Go to the beach'. **10** sits at the highest point of the fitness landscape.

The TSP example illustrates the same point. Here the problem can also be simply stated: 'What is the shortest tour?' Starting with a selection of randomly created, fifteen-bit genomes, each will represent a possible tour. Again, we need a separate program to evaluate the length of tour represented by each one; the shorter the length, the greater the fitness. Somewhere among those thousands of possible genomes is a string denoting the shortest tour, the peak of the fitness landscape.

SAQ 1.4

Using your own words, sum up the three basic elements of a GA.

ANSWER...

I came up with the following summary:

▶ genomes, strings of bits representing possible solutions to the problem in hand;

▶ a separate program, a fitness function, to evaluate each genome for its suitability as a solution, and thus assign it a place on the fitness landscape, the space of possible solutions, with the best (fittest) near the peaks, and the worst (least fit) in the valleys;

▶ an initial population of many genomes, with their bits randomly set.

I illustrated these two points with two simple problems: the going-to-the-beach 'problem' and the TSP.

So the biological concept of a genome can be turned into a simplified computer representation. These artificial genomes can then be tested by computer programs to measure their fitness as solutions to various problems, and thus their place in the fitness landscape. However, this can hardly be the end of the matter – we can produce random solutions encoded in genomes, but none of them might be the correct, or even useful, solutions. Suppose we still want to go to the beach, but our feeble computer has only generated two random genomes, say **00** and **11**. When we come to test these we find that neither solves the problem; the first represents night-time on the weekend; the second is daytime on a weekday. As you've already seen, the tour **000010100011001** is a useless TSP solution, and so might be the majority of the tours in a randomly generated set.

We could of course ask the computer to repeatedly create and test random genes until we find the correct genome. With our first example this would scarcely take terribly long. With only four possible genomes even the most sluggish computer would soon stumble upon the genome **10**. A five-city TSP could easily be solved this way, too. But, as you can readily see, this approach is only a form of brute-force search with a slightly novel form of representation, and with exactly the same drawbacks. What if there were a million possible genomes – or a trillion? In such cases, randomly picking and testing genomes would be even less rewarding than trying to win a lottery jackpot.

ACTIVITY 1.1

A first look

In this activity, you'll look at a demonstration GA to give you a first insight into how GAs work in practice. Activity 1.1 on the DVD points you in the direction of numerous GA sites and toolkits.

4.2   Introducing diversity

We reviewed Darwin's simple, elegant and powerful chain of reasoning in the answer to SAQ 1.1. I also identified a key step in this argument: step 3 – organisms vary. If all members of a species were identical to one another, and produced offspring identical to themselves, it's difficult to see how there could be any evolution at all. This is a completely static picture. But as soon as there is *variation* among members of a species, evolution becomes possible. Without *diversity*, there can be no evolutionary change.

Biologists have since proposed two major mechanisms by which diversity is introduced into populations of organisms, diversity which drives the process of evolution: they are **mutation** and reproduction by **crossover**.

Mutation

Sadly for lovers of comic books and science fiction, mutation is not really a process that gives people superpowers or produces men with the heads of flies: it is much more prosaic. Mutation refers to changes made to an organism's genes at any point in an organism's life. The majority of mutations are the result of the introduction of errors when DNA is copied, although some may be created by radiation, chemicals or other environmental factors. These errors may range from a failure to copy a single base correctly, to the (much less frequent) reversal of a series of bases, where, for instance the sequence **ACGT** is copied as **TGCA**. The haemophilia passed to the descendants of Queen Victoria was almost certainly the result of a mutation in Victoria herself; there is no historical evidence that either of her parents or their families suffered from the condition.

We know that the chance of errors being introduced during copying is extremely low. If the process were error prone then inheritance itself would be endangered. It is estimated that the error rate during DNA transcription is equivalent to misprinting one *letter* in nearly 300 000 *pages* of text. However, DNA is copied so frequently, and so much is copied each time, that errors are certain to occur.

The consequences of errors are unpredictable. Although the majority will be harmful to the organism, some will be neutral, having little effect, and a few will bring about benefits to the host organism – perhaps making their limbs slightly longer or more powerful than those of their fellows. A beneficial mutation gives the host a better (perhaps almost imperceptibly so) chance of surviving long enough to reproduce and to pass the mutation on to future generations. Over time, the beneficial mutation is likely to accumulate inside the breeding population – and the species will have evolved slightly. Given sufficient time – thousands or even millions of years – the population will evolve to a state in which it will no longer be able to interbreed with representatives of the original species. There will now be two species.

Reproduction and crossover

I've tiptoed prudishly around the subject for long enough – it is time for a straight talk about *sex* (and how it drives evolution). Mendel's experiments demonstrated that his pea plants were inheriting pairs of genes from their parents; a theory confirmed when pairs of chromosomes were first lined up on a microscope slide. Each of us obtains one copy of each chromosome from our father's sperm cell and a corresponding chromosome from our mother's egg. We might expect that we should be able to match each one of our chromosomes with an identical chromosome in one or other of our parents, but this is not the case – your chromosomes are completely unique.

This might seem to be something of a contradiction. I have already stated that our chromosomes come from our parents; yet they do not resemble those of our parents. What is happening? In fact, your parents' sperm and eggs were each created in a complex process known as **meiosis**, during which corresponding pairs of their chromosomes swapped genetic material in a process known as **crossover** or **recombination**, illustrated in Figure 1.5. Matching regions of each chromosome are repeatedly exchanged between chromosomes in a more-or-less random process, with the result that the original chromosomes are thoroughly scrambled; but because crossover almost always exchanges corresponding regions of DNA, each new chromosome contains all of the genes found in the parent.

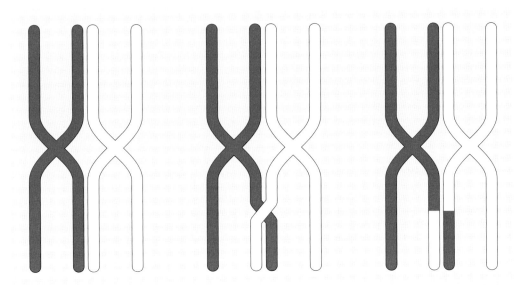

Figure 1.5   The three stages of crossover. Two X chromosomes line up alongside one another (left). Special proteins weaken part of the chromosome's DNA, allowing it to drift away from its host chromosome and line up alongside the neighbouring chromosome (middle). Finally, the DNA is grafted to its new chromosome (right)

The random nature of crossover ensures that every sperm cell and every egg cell has a unique set of chromosomes. Crossover explains why siblings (unless they are identical twins) are not exact copies of one another, yet show great similarities. After crossover, the chromosomes separate and the cell divides. Each of the new sex cells (they are called **gametes**) inherits only *one* set of chromosomes (i.e. half the total found in normal cells – in humans, sperm and eggs contain twenty-three chromosomes each). The full complement of chromosomes will only be restored when a sperm cell fuses with an egg cell to form a **zygote**, which will eventually develop into a new individual.

SAQ 1.5

Using your own words, briefly sum up the steps of the process through which a genetically unique new individual is formed.

ANSWER..

I have only skimmed the surface of a great deal of biological detail here, but I identified the following steps:

▶ In each parent, pairs of chromosomes line up and exchange genetic material, thus shuffling the genetic information. This process is called meiosis.

▶ The cells divide, creating gametes, each possessing only one of each pair of chromosomes. (A human gamete will thus contain only twenty-three out of the original forty-six chromosomes.)

▶ In reproduction, one gamete from one parent will fuse with one gamete from the other parent to form a zygote, possessing the full complement of chromosomes for that species. The zygote will go on to develop into a unique new individual.

It is now possible to alter DNA in adult organisms by introducing new DNA into cells, usually by deliberately infecting them with genetically engineered viruses. This controversial technology is known as *gene therapy* and has been trialled as a cure for various inherited conditions caused by single defective genes. So far it has had mixed results.

No organism has control over the genes it inherits from its parents. It will flourish or fail depending on the combination of genes in the single egg and sperm from which it developed. In turn, it has no control over which genes will be included in its sex cells; crossover guarantees randomness, ensuring diversity within the gene pool.

You may be wondering why crossover occurs at all. It does seem to complicate matters, but in reality it is vital to avoid species becoming extinct. Mutations are usually harmful, negatively affecting the health of the host organism. If they were allowed to accumulate in the gene pool they would eventually drive the species to extinction. Without crossover, harmful mutations could only be eliminated in one of two ways:

1 by a back mutation which would have the effect of reversing the original mutation;

2 by a second, compensating mutation occurring elsewhere on the genome.

Mutations occur at random, so it is incredibly unlikely that the next mutation would be a back mutation, and would be much more likely to be a harmful one at another location on the genome. Succeeding generations would carry more and more mutations, becoming less capable of surviving. Recombination allows mutated parental genes to be excluded from the chromosomes passed to children: they do not inexorably accumulate in the gene pool; the species remains healthy and diverse.

4.3 Driving evolution

We now have the components of a GA in place – the genome, a fitness function, an initial population – and we have two ways to keep our genomes diverse. So what now? You've already learned that the idea of a GA is to evolve solutions to a problem. The genomes are potential solutions. How do GAs mimic the processes of Darwinian evolution to achieve this? They use the following three-step process: starting with our initial population of genomes (I will call this population **Generation 1**) with randomised bits, they:

1 generate a mating pool;

2 create a new population (Generation 2);

3 return to step 2.

Let's now look at these steps in detail. I'll work through an unrealistic, but very simple, example – an optimisation problem: what is the maximum score possible from rolling two conventional six-sided dice? (*We* may know that the value is 12, achieved by rolling two 6s, but the GA would not 'know' this fact.)

The dice are represented using a genome with two genes, one for each dice (see Figure 1.6). We can represent each die using three bits (capable of holding values between 0 and 7 which is more than enough for the possible values from 1 to 6); therefore our genome will contain a total of six bits.

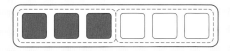

Figure 1.6   A genome consisting of two genes, each of three bits. The different values of the bits are shown by their colour – colour = 0, white = 1

Making it to the mating pool

At the beginning of our experiment the population contains random dice genomes. Table 1.4 shows four examples, with the fittest genome (i.e. the one producing the highest score) highlighted in grey.

Table 1.4

	Die 1 value	Die 1 binary	Die 2 value	Die 2 binary	Genome
A	1	001	5	101	**001101**
B	6	110	4	100	**110100**
C	3	011	4	100	**011100**
D	4	100	4	100	**100100**

The genomes are then passed through a fitness function. In this case, since we are looking for the maximum sum for the two dice, our fitness function will simply add the values of the two dice; the result will be the **fitness value** for each genome (see Table 1.5); those genomes with higher values are said to be *fitter* than those with lower values. The fitter the genome, the better the solution it represents.

Table 1.5

Genome	Genome value	Die 1 value	Die 2 value	Fitness value
A	**001101**	1	5	6
B	**110100**	6	4	10
C	**011100**	3	4	7
D	**100100**	4	4	8

From the table above, it can be seen that genome **B** is the fittest with a score of 10, whilst genome **A** is the least fit, scoring only 6. The fitness value directly influences the likelihood of a genome going through to later rounds of the simulation. Those with high fitness values are more likely to survive; those that are least fit are more likely to be discarded. The genes selected for survival will enter a **mating pool** from which future generations can be bred.

The actual method for choosing the fittest genomes is left up to the GA designer. The simplest is to exclusively select the genes with the highest fitness values and discard the rest. However, there are good reasons to prefer a more subtle strategy and to introduce an element of randomness into the selection, thus maintaining diversity inside the gene pool. The method will be one that generally selects the fittest genomes, but gives a relatively unsuccessful genome some chance of passing into the mating pool.

One such method is the **biased roulette wheel** method. The metaphor is of the spinning wheel edged with either thirty-seven or thirty-eight slots used in the well-known casino game. Roulette players lay stakes on particular colours or numbers being selected at random: a small ball, thrown into the spinning wheel, bounces around at random and comes to rest in one of the slots – whereupon most people lose their money.

The GA 'roulette wheel' is a similar idea. It will have a number of slots, one for each genome in the population. And although in conventional roulette each slot has an equal chance of being selected, the GA wheel is *biased* towards slots representing genomes with fitter values. A percentage of the wheel is allocated to each of the genomes. Those genomes with the higher fitness values have greater percentages of the wheel. The percentages are calculated by dividing the fitness value of each genome by the total fitnesses of all of the genomes and expressing the value as a percentage.

For our four genomes the percentages are as shown in the pie chart in Table 1.6.

Table 1.6

Genome	Fitness value	Percentage*	
A	6		
B	10	32.3 (equivalent to 10/31 × 100%)	
C	7		
D	8	25.8	
Total	31	100	

* Percentages have been rounded in this table; the computer would use a far higher accuracy.

SAQ 1.6

Fill in the percentages of the wheel allocated to genomes **A** and **C**.

ANSWER..

A has 19.4% of the wheel (6/31 × 100); **C** has 22.6% (7/31 × 100).

An unbiased wheel would have given all four genes an equal chance, with each receiving 25%.

The wheel is now 'spun' once for each of the genomes, and the result recorded. For our set of genomes, we will have to spin it four times. The spin is simulated by using a random number generator to produce 'random' values from 0 to 100 (representing percentages). If the random number generator produces a value between 0 and 19.4 then **A** will enter the mating pool, if it produces a value between 19.4 and 51.7

In reality the numbers produced by random number generators are not truly random – they are termed *pseudo-random* numbers.

(a range of 32.3%) then **B** will be chosen, and so on. Table 1.7 shows the results for four spins of the 'wheel'.

Table 1.7

Spin	Selected genome
1	**A**
2	**D**
3	**B**
4	**B**

As you can see from the results, our most successful genome (**B**) has been selected twice. Two copies of **B** will enter the mating pool. The random nature of the wheel can be discerned in the fact that the relatively strong genome **C** was not selected for the mating pool; whilst the relatively weak genome **A** has been chosen. Clearly, then, the roulette wheel does not *guarantee* the elimination of weak genomes – it is possible (although unlikely) that no copies of the strongest genome will pass into the mating pool and that genome would be eliminated. Generally speaking, though, the pool should consist of genomes with a higher average fitness than that of the original population, with the fittest genomes being most strongly represented.

Once the mating pool has been generated, the algorithm then moves to the next step: populating the next generation.

Generating a new population

The mating pool is now used to create a new population of genomes. A series of 'dips' is made into the pool. Pairs of genomes are selected at random (although not removed from the pool). The dipping process continues until the number of genomes selected equals that of the previous generation. In our example above, there were four genomes in the initial population, so two dips must be made into the mating pool (see Table 1.8).

Table 1.8

Dip	Genomes selected
1	**A** and **B**
2	**B** and **A**

Once again, the randomness of the dipping process means there is no guarantee that only strong genomes will be selected from the pool. You will notice from the diagram above that although the relatively successful genome **D** was present in the mating pool, it was *not* selected; therefore genome **D** will not take part in forming the new population. **B** was the most populous genome in the mating pool, making its selection most likely.

A GA tends to preferentially discard weaker genomes from the population, while retaining stronger ones. No matter how many genomes were created originally, repeating the process of:

1   applying the fitness function;

2   spinning the roulette wheel;

3   dipping, to form a mating pool;

would eventually result in the entire population being represented by just one or two genomes from the original population. It is quite likely that these would be some of the fittest genomes present amongst the original, random population; but we can be less sure that they are the fittest genomes *possible*. The random process responsible for creating the genomes may have chanced upon the fittest genome at the very start, but in a complex problem this is highly unlikely.

To ensure that we find the fittest possible genome we must create a new population of genomes based upon the relatively successful genomes chosen from the mating pool. We have to create *diversity*. Without diversity there can be no evolution, and our genomes will need to evolve by crossover and by mutation.

Evolving genomes by crossover ...

Most GAs permit crossover of genes between genomes. Genes have a certain probability of crossing over known as the *crossover rate*. The crossover rate can be thought of as rolling a particular number on a die along the lines of 'if a 6 is rolled, then this pair of genes will cross over'. If we roll a number other than 6 then the two genomes pass unaltered into the new population (as shown in Figure 1.7).

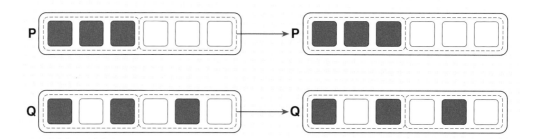

Figure 1.7   The parent genomes P and Q do not cross over. Instead they pass to the next generation without any alterations

If, however, a 6 is rolled, then the two genes cross over. The two parent genomes are split at a random point along their length and the first part of each gene is swapped with its partner. Two new child genomes are created as a result, each inheriting a proportion of its genes from each of its parent genomes, as illustrated in Figure 1.8. These two offspring then pass into the new population.

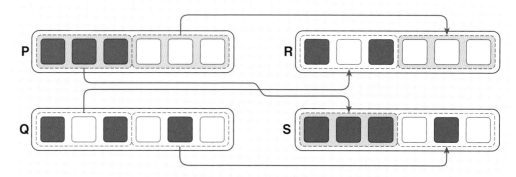

Figure 1.8   Crossover between two genomes. In this case, the parent genomes P and Q split between their two genes at point 3 (between their third and fourth bits). The child genome R inherits its first gene from Q and its second from P; child genome S inherits its first gene from P and its second from Q

As the dipping process is random, a parent genome may be selected from the mating pool a number of times; each time the dice will be rolled to determine whether crossover with its partner is to happen: sometimes it will cross and produce new children, at other times it will pass into the child pool unaltered. It is entirely possible that a parent genome will exist in the child pool alongside its own children.

SAQ 1.7

Genes **A** (**011011**) and **B** (**111010**) are selected for crossover at point 2. What will their children be?

ANSWER..

The children will be **111011** and **011010**. **A** and **B** just exchange their first two bits.

Crossover creates large changes in genomes between generations; it is therefore an excellent method of introducing widespread diversity into the gene pool. The rate of crossover directly influences the rate at which the pool diversifies – a low rate slows diversification, a high rate encourages it. The rate of crossover is chosen by the designer of the simulation. Our rate of 1/6 is probably too low for most purposes; a rate of approximately 1/2 is an acceptable compromise.

... and by mutation

Some GAs also promote diversity by incorporating *mutation*. Just as biological genomes are subject to copying and other errors, so it is possible to introduce errors into software genomes. Whilst crossover introduces gross changes into the genome, mutation is responsible for minor changes. However, minor changes may have very large consequences for the genome's fitness.

If the GA designer decides to permit mutation of genomes, it is generally agreed that the process must be relatively rare. Over-frequent mutation can result in fit genomes being destroyed by random changes to their contents. This slows the evolutionary process, effectively resetting the clock and preventing the population from converging on an optimal solution. Conversely, though, the mutation rate should be sufficiently high to maintain diversity within the population. Mutations in the genome help prevent stagnation around local optima and increase the likelihood of the genome finding the truly optimal solution.

The GA designer sets a *mutation rate* that remains constant throughout the simulation. Again, the mutation rate may be thought of as rolling a die with a rule such as 'if a 6 is rolled, then mutate this gene'. Then each genome is selected in turn and the die rolled. Any number from 1 to 5 and no mutation occurs. However, if a 6 comes up then we apply the mutation rule. In reality, the mutation rate would usually be much lower than 1/6. Most GAs generally use very low levels of mutation, relying instead on crossover to generate diversity. However, recent work suggests that mutation may be a more potent means of ensuring diversity and convergence than crossover.

The exact type of mutation depends on the simulation, but in our present simple example we'll just say that a mutation affects one, randomly chosen, gene in the genome, and that the effect of the mutation is to flip the value of the gene from coloured to white (1 to 0) and vice versa: white to coloured (0 to 1). Other GA programs might use decimal numbers or strings in their genomes and will require different mutation operations, such as replacing the mutated gene with a new random value.

The problem of local optima is universal in optimisation problems. You'll recall it has come up many times already in M366, notably in relation to PSO (Block 3) and Hopfield networks (Block 4).

The designer must also choose a point in the algorithm at which mutation should occur: this is generally either when genomes are selected from the mating pool (see Figure 1.9) or during a crossover (see Figure 1.10). Most commonly, mutation is introduced during crossover.

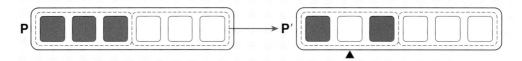

Figure 1.9   The mutation of a single gene in a genome during selection. A genome has been chosen for mutation: one of its genes is selected at random and is mutated. Here, the second gene in **P** (indicated by the small triangle below the gene) has its value reversed from coloured to white. From now on I'll use the 'prime' notation **P′** to indicate that the gene **P** has been mutated

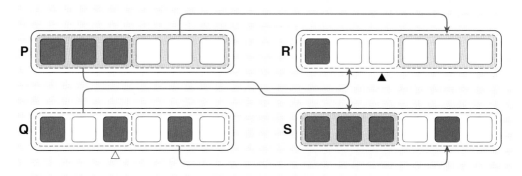

Figure 1.10   Mutation during crossover. In this example, genome **Q** has been chosen for mutation. The third gene from genome **Q** (indicated by the small triangle below the gene) is flipped from coloured to white during crossover ending up in the new child genome **R′**. (You will see that the third gene of **R′** is white, an attribute absent from both of the parent genomes **P** and **Q**.)

The new set of genes resulting from the transfer, crossover and mutation of genes in the mating pool now becomes the new population. The old population, Generation 1, is deleted and our new set becomes Generation 2.

Now repeat the process

GAs rarely reach a solution in a single generation. Just as the wealth and diversity of the natural world is the result of unimaginably large numbers of tiny, incremental changes, the end result of a GA is the accumulation of changes over many tens, hundreds or even thousands of generations.

After the new population (Generation 2) has been created from the mating pool, it is time to start again. Going back to step 1, the algorithm applies the fitness function to the new population, spins the roulette wheel, creates a mating pool, then creates another new population (Generation 3) – and so on. Neither crossover nor mutation are guaranteed to occur: it is entirely possible that the new population will consist solely of genes from the previous population. As time passes, however, crossover and mutation *will* take place. New genomes *will* appear in the population. Some of these will be stronger than their predecessors from earlier generations, and the numbers of such fit genomes will increase at the expense of weaker strains. As the generations pass, it is likely that none of the original genomes will remain, having been replaced wholesale by their stronger children. Likewise the average fitness of the population will increase, inching towards the solution of the problem.

You've just read through quite a complex series of steps. Let's try to sum these up and consolidate them in your minds with the following short series of questions and exercises.

SAQ 1.8

Sum up in your own words the stages through which a GA passes in evolving the genome population. Look back if you need to.

ANSWER...

Here is a brief summary of the steps. At Generation n:

1 Create a mating pool of the same size as the population by:
  - 1.i applying the fitness function to every genome;
  - 1.ii randomly selecting genomes from the population, based on the biased roulette wheel;
  - 1.iii mutating genes in the mating pool (alternatively, mutation may occur at the step 2.iii, or not at all).
2 Build a new population (Generation $n+1$) by:
  - 2.i selecting pairs of genomes in the mating pool for crossover (those not selected pass directly into the new population);
  - 2.ii mutating genes on crossover (alternatively, mutation may occur at step 1.iii, or not at all).
3 Go back to step 1.

This process is repeated until very good solutions emerge.

It's worth making a special point of how great a part *randomness* plays in the whole process, pictured in our account above as the roll of a die (in reality, the generation of a random number by the computer).

SAQ 1.9

Note down the various points at which the decision of the GA is made randomly. Look back if you need to.

ANSWER...

I identified the following points at which the GA makes random decisions:

▶ the selection of genomes for the mating pool by means of the biased roulette wheel;
▶ the selection of genomes for crossover;
▶ the selection of the crossover point;
▶ the selection of genomes for mutation;
▶ the selection of the mutated gene.

Finally, to pull things together, consider the following exercise.

Exercise 1.2

Assume that the population at Generation *n* of our dice simulation is made up of the following six genomes:

A 011011
B 100110
C 001110
D 110101
E 100100
F 001001

Work through another round of the algorithm to generate a new population for Generation *n*+1. Assume a crossover rate of 3/6 and mutation rate of 2/6. Generate your own random numbers where necessary – you can throw a die if you have one to hand. To simplify matters slightly, mutate genomes in the mating pool, not on crossover.

Discussion ....

First of all, we need to apply the fitness function to each of the six genomes, as shown in Table 1.9.

Table 1.9

Genome	Genome value	Die 1	Die 2	Fitness
A	011011	3	3	6
B	100110	4	6	10
C	001110	1	6	7
D	110101	6	5	11
E	100100	4	4	8
F	001001	1	1	2

Total fitness				44
Mean fitness				7.33

I used these values to set up a biased roulette wheel (see Figure 1.11).

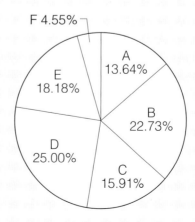

Figure 1.11 The biased roulette wheel

I then spun the wheel six times (once for each genome), generating a random number between 1 and 100 each time (see Table 1.10).

Table 1.10

Spin	Result	Genome selected
1	38	C
2	94	E
3	65	D
4	44	C
5	62	D
6	11	A

You will have got different results, of course. Note that, although the relatively strong genome **D** was selected twice, so was the relatively weak genome **C**. That's randomness for you.

Now, we've decided to apply the mutation operation at this step, so I threw the die six times, getting 4, 1, 4, 6, 3 and 4. This means that I just had to mutate the genome in the fourth row of the table above, **C** (**001110**). I got my research assistant to throw the die again, the result was 2, so I flipped the second gene in this genome, giving me **011110**. So my mating pool now consisted of these six genomes:

  C   **001110**
  E   **100100**
  D   **110101**
  C′ **011110**
  D   **110101**
  A   **011011**

The next step was to build Generation $n+1$ from the mating pool. First of all, I dipped into the mating pool six times, giving me three pairs of genomes that may (or may not) mate. I got:

  Threw 3 and 4   Pair 1   **110101** (**D**) and **011110** (**C′**)
  Threw 6 and 4   Pair 2   **011011** (**A**) and **011110** (**C′**)
  Threw 3 and 4   Pair 3   **110101** (**D**) and **011110** (**C′**)

Again, **C** looks over-represented, but this time in its mutated form. Remembering that the crossover rate is 1/2, I then threw the die three times to determine which, if any, of the three pairs would mate. If the throw is 3 or under, then there is no crossover and both genomes pass unaltered into the next generation; a throw of 4, 5 or 6 means that the pair crosses over. This time the results were:

  Threw   4   Pair 1   **D** and **C′** cross over
  Threw   3   Pair 2   **A** and **C′** go into Generation $n+1$
  Threw   1   Pair 3   **D** and **C′** go into Generation $n+1$

So I had to cross over **D** and **C′**. To do this I needed to throw the die one more time to find the crossover point. The die came up 2, so:

  110101 and **011110**

cross over between the second and third genes, giving:

  010101 and **111110**

So my population of genomes in Generation *n*+1 was as shown in Table 1.11.

Table 1.11

Genome	Genome value	Die 1	Die 2	Fitness
A	011011	3	3	6
C'	011110	3	6	9
D	110101	6	5	11
C'	011110	3	6	9
G	010101	2	5	8
H	111110	6	6	12
Total fitness				55
Mean fitness				9.17

Note that I'm counting 111 (7) as 6; and I would have counted 000 (0) as 1. You can easily see that the average fitness of the population has risen – you might have had a different result: there is no guarantee that the fitness will rise in a single generation, of course, as the process depends on so many random events. In this case the total fitness has risen from 44 to 55 whilst the mean fitness has noticeably improved from 7.33 to 9.17.

Nevertheless, the mean fitness should rise inexorably over many generations. You will have also observed that genome **H**, representing the highest possible throw has entered the population for the first time.

This, then, is the basic structure of a GA. You can probably relate the model to the biological theories on which it is based. I'll return to this point shortly. For the moment, though, let's consider a few of the variations and improvements on the basic pattern that have come out of the research community in recent years.

4.4 Variations on a theme

The example given above was an extremely simple demonstration of how a GA works. Researchers have continued to modify the basic algorithm to yield superior performance. I'll now consider briefly five of these modifications.

Elitism

The simple algorithm discussed above has a significant drawback; it does not protect fit genomes nearly strongly enough. As you've learned, a genome with a high fitness value can be lost in a number of ways: it might never be selected by the roulette wheel; it might fail to be selected from the mating pool; or its advantageous make-up might be lost in an unfortunate crossover or through a mutation.

One method of overcoming this is to cheat somewhat and indulge in **elitism**, ensuring that a certain proportion of high-scoring genomes *always* enter the next generation unscathed. This policy may forsake some of the purity of the original biological inspiration, but it has been shown to improve the performance of GAs significantly.

Two-point crossover

As you learned from the very brief discussion of meiosis above, crossover in living organisms is not necessarily confined to a single point along a chromosome. For example, in a **two-point crossover** the middle section of a chromosome may cross over and find itself sandwiched in the middle of a new gene. It is possible to amend the crossover process in a GA to mimic this (see Figure 1.12).

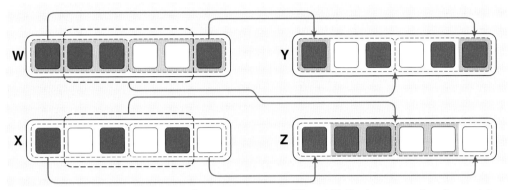

Figure 1.12   A two-point crossover between genomes **W** and **X**. Each genome has two points of crossover – between genes 1 and 2 and between 5 and 6. The middle section of each genome finds a new home in the middle of genomes **Y** and **Z**

I will return to this point in the next unit, when I discuss *schemas*.

Changing the selection pressure

In our simple example above, I was ruthless with the less-well-performing genomes; they were given relatively little chance of progressing to future generations. But for many problem domains this policy can often lead quickly to a population with far too little variability – and variation is essential for successful evolution. Imagine a search space in which there is some variability between genomes, some being slightly better adapted than others, but none of which are close to ideal. Rapidly reducing the variability of the population will thus restrict the area of the landscape covered by the genomes. Crossover and mutation might reintroduce diversity into the population, but this may take a long time, and there is no guarantee that it will happen at all.

An alternative strategy, known as **Boltzmann selection**, begins with a relatively low rate of selection, with weaker strains being given a greater chance of being selected for future generations, thus allowing the search space to be more thoroughly covered. As time passes, the selection rate becomes more intense, weaker genomes being progressively eliminated from the population, and the surviving genomes finally converging on optimal, or very near optimal, solutions.

Real-numbered genomes

So far, I've been considering genomes that are bit strings, simple sequences of 1s and 0s. But scientists and engineers are accustomed to working with *real numbers*. Of course it is possible to represent a real number as a string of bits, but it is rather tedious to have to do so, and it may mean very long genomes (and thus much more work for the computer) in a GA applied to a real-world problem. Some GA designers therefore prefer to work with genomes that are strings of real numbers, as in Figure 1.13.

Figure 1.13 Example of a real-numbered genome

This has been rather a controversial issue in the GA community, but I don't propose to discuss any of the arguments here. There is only one point that does need to be clarified: how do real-number genomes cross over? One simple and obvious strategy is illustrated in Figure 1.14, where two genomes are represented as crossing before point 3.

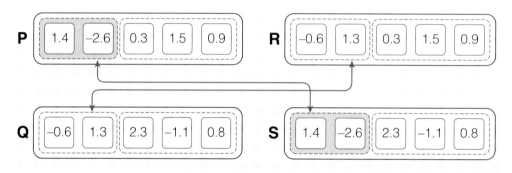

Figure 1.14 Example of two real-numbered genomes crossing over

A rather more subtle strategy – perhaps more suitable to problems in which the solutions are combinations of real numbers – is known as **arithmetical crossover**. For two genomes **A** and **B**, it works like this:

▶ generate a random number β in the range 0–1;

▶ multiply each gene in **A** by β, giving **A**′;

▶ multiply each gene in **B** by $(1 - \beta)$, giving **B**′;

▶ add each element of **A**′ to the corresponding element of **B**′, giving the new crossed-over genome.

See the Maths Guide for linear combinations.

Picturing **A** and **B** as *vectors* **a** and **b**, this amounts to a linear combination of **a** and **b**, giving a new vector **c**:

$$\mathbf{c} = \beta\mathbf{a} + (1 - \beta)\mathbf{b} \qquad (1.1)$$

This process is carried out twice, giving two identical children. Try an example.

SAQ 1.10

Consider the genomes **A** = {1.40 –2.60 0.30 1.50 0.90} and **B** = {–0.60 1.30 2.30 –1.10 0.80}. What is the result of arithmetical crossover, given a value of β = 0.4?

ANSWER..

Multiplying **A** by 0.4 and **B** by (1 – 0.4) = 0.6, we get **A**′ = {0.56 –1.04 0.12 0.60 0.36} and **B**′ = {–0.36 0.78 1.38 –0.66 0.48}. Adding the two, we get the new genome **C** = **A**′ + **B**′ = {0.2 –0.26 1.50 –0.06 0.84}.

It is also possible to combine this idea with that of a crossover *point*, in which case the arithmetical operation above would only happen to the genes before the crossover point, the other genes remaining unchanged in both children.

Multi-objective GAs

Almost all the optimisation problems I've considered in M366, problems like the TSP, are what are known as **single-objective** problems. It should be clear what this means: there is just one feature we want to optimise. In the TSP, this is simply the length of the tour. For an engine designer, it might be the best fuel efficiency; for a biochemist, the lowest energy configuration of a protein; for a materials engineer, an alloy of maximum strength, and so on. But many real-world problems are more complex than this: they are **multi-objective**. To take the engine design example again, an incredibly fuel-efficient design might be too costly to make, or too heavy, or too large. The materials engineer might find a super-strong alloy that was made out of elements so rare that it could never be produced. So in many cases we are looking not for the optimum of a single feature f, but for the optima of a whole group of inter-related features f_1, f_2, f_3 ... f_n. And since generally there will be trade-offs between most of these features, there is not going to be any single solution combining the maxima of all of them. Rather, there will be a range of solutions, each representing a *compromise* among the various features we want to optimise: a slightly lighter, but still very strong, alloy, for instance; or a cheaper engine with a bit less than the best fuel efficiency.

GA techniques exist for tackling multi-objective problems. Going into the detail of them would take us beyond the scope of M366, but usually they involve either devising complex fitness functions or dividing the population of genomes into sub-populations, each responsible for optimising a single feature. Part of Case Study 1.2 below deals with a multi-objective problem.

Now let's sum up the main theoretical lessons of the unit in the following exercise.

SAQ 1.11

Draw up a table with features of biological theory that we have covered in the unit in the left-hand column and the corresponding artificial property of a GA in the right-hand column.

ANSWER...

I came up with Table 1.12.

Table 1.12 Corresponding features of biological theory and GAs

Biological feature	GA feature
Natural selection	Selection for mating pool based on a fitness function
DNA	Artificial genomes
Meiosis	Crossover
Mutation	Random mutation of bits

As you can see, and as so often in biologically inspired computing, the resemblance is only superficial. Artificial computational models are always simplifications of a complex reality.

As with neural networks, computing researchers are often uncomfortable with the use of biological terminology to describe features of computational models. Just as artificial neurons are often referred to by the more neutral word 'units', so artificial genomes are often termed **bit strings**. I will use this term at times throughout the remainder of the block.

Computer Exercises 1.1 to 1.5

In these exercises, you'll look at a demonstration GA tool and use it to explore how GAs work in practice. On the course DVD, find and work through Computer Exercises 1.1 to 1.5.

5 The power of genetic algorithms

Let's now end this unit by looking fairly informally at two areas in which GAs have been successfully applied.

Case Study 1.1: Strategy

The **Prisoner's Dilemma** is a deceptively simple 'game', formulated in 1950 by Merrill Flood and Melvin Dresher at the RAND Institute, which has continued to infuriate researchers ever since. The premise of the game is extremely straightforward: two suspects (called A and B) are arrested and thrown into separate prison cells. Each is then given a choice – they can testify against the other prisoner (they are said to *defect*) or they can remain silent (they *cooperate*). Each prisoner potentially has something to gain and lose from their choice. The rules are these:

▶ If a prisoner defects and the other prisoner cooperates then the defector will go free and the cooperator will be imprisoned for ten years.

▶ If neither prisoner defects then they both automatically receive a short sentence of six months.

▶ If both prisoners defect then each receives a two-year sentence.

The rules are summed up in Table 1.13.

Table 1.13 Sentences awarded in the Prisoner's Dilemma

	Prisoner B cooperates	Prisoner B defects
Prisoner A cooperates	Both serve six months	Prisoner A serves ten years; Prisoner B goes free
Prisoner A defects	Prisoner A goes free; Prisoner B serves ten years	Both serve two years

Since the two prisoners cannot communicate with one another they must each decide what to do by guessing at the behaviour of the other.

A first guess might be that it always pays to behave unscrupulously and for one prisoner to betray the other; but, as the table above demonstrates, if both prisoners betray one another the punishment for both is worse than if both had remained silent. In fact, it is better for both prisoners to stay quiet – but there is always a temptation to defect.

Played for a single round, the Prisoner's Dilemma is hardly very interesting: the game can be 'won' if one player defects but the other cooperates. However, it becomes a fascinating problem if the challenge is repeated time and time again in the game of **Iterated Prisoner's Dilemma**, first suggested by Richard Axelrod in 1984. In this version of the game each player has a *memory* of previous rounds, which they can use to guide future decisions. Each player's aim is to minimise the amount of jail time they accumulate through the game.

Axelrod organised a number of tournaments to attempt to decide what was the best strategy that could be adopted. Programs submitted to the tournaments ranged from very complex systems based on Bayesian analysis, through to very simple ones, such as just deciding randomly. Strangely, it emerged that by far the most successful strategy was one called TITFORTAT. As its name suggests, the first move in this approach is to cooperate, and in remaining rounds do exactly what the opponent has just done.

After two tournaments, Axelrod applied a GA system to the problem, to see if it could evolve better strategies than TITFORTAT. A fitness function based on analysis of successful strategies submitted to the tournaments was applied to a population of seventy-bit genomes (and thus producing a search space of 2^{70} possible strategies). The simulation followed the pattern I've outlined above. It was run forty times, each time for fifty generations. The results were instructive: the GA developed strategies very similar to TITFORTAT, some of which scored even more highly than TITFORTAT itself.

You might be wondering what is the point of Prisoner's Dilemma. In fact, it has major implications in many fields of study. It has become one of the foundation stones of what has come to be called **game theory**, one classic application of which has been to the political question of arms races, such as during the Cold War. In an arms race, each country can choose to increase expenditure on weapons or to enter into arms reduction agreements. However, both parties will be uncertain that the other will honour the terms of such agreements: if one destroys weapons whilst the other re-arms, then the strategic balance will be upset. In such conditions there is an almost inexorable pressure to build more and more weapons.

Prisoner's Dilemma has also been used to investigate such diverse phenomena as advertising campaigns among competing cigarette manufacturers and the behaviour of competitors in the Tour de France. Most tellingly, perhaps, it has been applied to biological questions, such as the evolution of cooperation amongst animals. I have given some further information and links on the course DVD and the course website.

Case Study 1.2: Aircraft wing design

One area where GAs show real industrial potential is in the design of aircraft wings. Superficially, wings might just appear to be simple strips of metal with few moving parts, but they are actually one of the greatest design challenges of an aircraft.

Aircraft wing design

Any powered aircraft, from a simple engine-driven hang-glider to the monstrous new double-decker A380 Airbus, stays in the air by virtue of the same principles. Four key forces act on a plane: *weight*, *lift*, *thrust* and *drag* (see Figure 1.15). Two of these work in favour of flight, and two against it. Naturally, the *weight* of a plane continually pulls it back down to earth under gravity; but *lift* is an upward force, generated by the plane's wing, making it airborne. *Thrust* is the force created by the engines, pushing the plane forward and making lift possible through the flow of air over the wing surfaces; but *drag*, which arises from the friction of the plane as it butts through the air, works in the opposite direction, pulling the plane backwards and slowing it down. Powered flight is a constant battle among these four forces. Lift has to overpower weight, and thrust dominate drag, for the plane to fly at all.

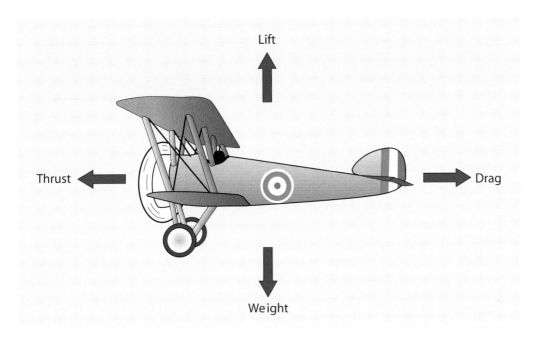

Figure 1.15 The four key forces acting on an aeroplane

Crucial to all this is the wing. Obviously, the design of the engines, the materials and shape of the fuselage, and the overall dimensions, capacity and purpose of the plane are significant; but it is the wing that generates the all-important lift and is a major source of drag. The design of the wing is clearly a problem in optimisation – the engineer's most important objective is to maximise lift and minimise drag. This is clearly a *single-objective optimisation problem*: to make the ratio of lift to drag as high as possible. But there are other factors to consider as well. Generally speaking, a larger, deeper wing will generate more lift than a smaller, thinner one, and it will also hold more fuel. However, a thick wing will be heavier and require more powerful (and thus heavier) engines to generate the necessary thrust. Issues of cost, structural strength and the ability to flatten out shockwaves also come into the equation. Stated like this, the design of an aircraft wing then comes down to a *multi-objective optimisation problem*.

Finding the optimal configuration of an aircraft wing can generally be done in two design stages:

▶ First, the basic shape of the wing – sometimes called its *planform* – is usually fixed early in the design process, as many other design and cost considerations flow from this choice. A few possible planforms are illustrated in Figure 1.16(a), although there is an infinite range of variations on each of these basic structures.

▶ Much more subtle is the precise shaping of the wing within the agreed planform. Lift is generated by the flow of air over the curved surfaces of the aerofoil – a cross-section of a typical wing is shown in Figure 1.16(b). Here, even tiny variations in angles and widths can make immense differences in the lifting capacity and drag produced by the wing.

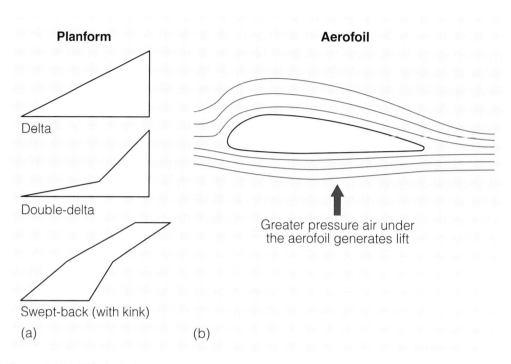

Figure 1.16 (a) Typical wing planforms. (b) Typical wing cross-section

Usually, wing design is a process of trial and error, backed up with a lot of heavy mathematics and plenty of wind-tunnel testing. But since GAs are used so widely in optimisation, there is no reason why they should not be applied here. A group of Japanese researchers and engineers, associated with Tokohu University and NASA, and working on the design for a NASA supersonic transport plane, have done exactly this.

If you want to read about this in more detail, see Obayasha et al. (2000) and Oyama (2000).

As in any GA approach, the first task is to find a way to express potential solutions to the problem as numerical sequences – strings of either bits or real numbers. It's not immediately obvious how this can be done, but in fact both the design of the planform and of the aerofoil can be expressed exactly in a fairly small number of numerical *design parameters*: six for the planform and ten for a single section through the wing. Figure 1.17(a) shows the parameters for the planform and 1.17(b) for the cross-section. (Figure 1.17(b) illustrates a system known as PARSEC.) To fix the exact shape of the aerofoil it is necessary to specify the parameters for several cross-sections along the wing's entire length.

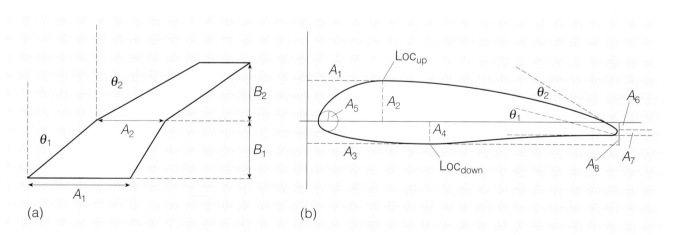

Figure 1.17 Design parameters for (a) planform. (b) aerofoil cross-section

There are several possible variations on this approach.

Let's now briefly examine two experiments in which evolutionary algorithms were successfully applied to the problem.

Single-objective optimisation: evolving an aerofoil with maximum *L/D*

Working with the predetermined planform similar to the swept-back formation in Figure 1.16(a) and using the PARSEC design parameter model illustrated in Figure 1.17(b), Akira Oyama used a GA to evolve an aerofoil in which the ratio of lift *L* to drag *D* was a maximum. He took seven sections across the wing, characterising each section by ten of the eleven PARSEC design parameters. With further parameters to describe each section's location, angle of attack and other key features, he was thus able to specify a population of potential aerofoils using a total of eighty-seven parameters, and thus of real-number genomes, each of length eighty-seven.

Some of the variations on the basic GA procedures used by Oyama are beyond the scope of M366. Basically, however, he used elitism and a form of selection based on the ordering of the genomes' fitness, coupled with an averaging crossover scheme and a mutation probability of 10%. The fitness of each potential solution was assessed using the function:

The term *elitism* was introduced in Section 4.4 of this unit.

$$fitness = \begin{cases} 100 + L/D & \text{if } t \le t_{min} \\ (100 + L/D)e^{t-t_{min}} & \text{otherwise} \end{cases}$$

where t and t_{min} are terms for the thickness and minimum thickness of the wing at this point. The exponential term in the 'otherwise' part of the function heavily penalises unfit solutions.

Of course, to evaluate this, the *L* and *D* of each potential solution had to be calculated. This could be done purely mathematically, but involved enormous computational effort, even for a single potential aerofoil design. Fortunately, all the potential solutions in each generation could be evaluated in parallel, so Oyama was able to use a 166-processor, specialised parallel supercomputer, the *Numerical Wind Tunnel*. This brought computation time down from half a year on a conventional machine, to about four and a half days.

Oyama's final generation of solutions had a very satisfactory *L/D* ratio of 18.91. However, he points out that does not necessarily mean that a plane carrying such a wing would fly well. The wing might be too heavy, it might be too costly, it might be too weak; many other factors might affect its airworthiness. All this pointed to the need for a multi-objective approach.

Multi-objective optimisation: optimising *L/D* and weight

Using a multi-objective evolutionary algorithm, Oyama then aimed to evolve aerofoil designs that would minimise the drag, at the same time as minimising weight. As you learned earlier in this unit, multi-objective algorithms do not produce a single solution, but a set of possible solutions from which a winner can be selected by hand, based on the relative importance of the objectives. Figure 1.18 shows the range of solutions he obtained, with a Boeing 747's actual performance marked in for comparison

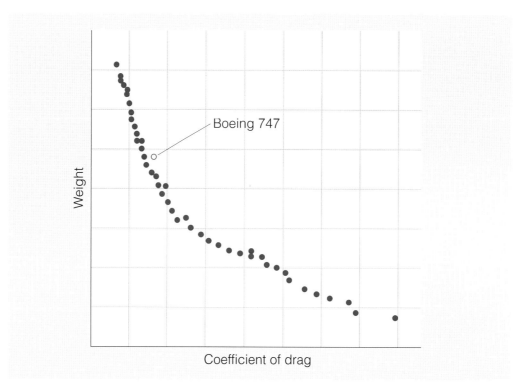

Figure 1.18

Once again, owing to the intensive mathematical calculations required, made harder in this experiment by the need for weight estimations, the GA had to be run on a parallel supercomputer.

6 Summary of Unit 1

I've had two main aims in this unit. The first is to cover as informally as possible the basic biological background that is the inspiration for GAs. I recalled the basic points of Darwin's theory and outlined the modern biochemical ideas that give us a fuller view of how evolution may work. I pointed out that Darwin lacked a fully worked-out theory of heredity – the workings of the DNA molecule underlie such a theory; and I have tried to give you a useful, although superficial, account of these, in the model of the gene and the genome.

The concepts of evolution and of the gene come together in GAs. Our second aim was to provide quite an extensive coverage of the basic principles of the GA. To this end, I had to go into a fair amount of detail. Some of this may have seemed somewhat overwhelming to start with; but the main outlines should now be clear. A GA solves a problem by:

1   starting with an initial random population of genomes, or bit strings, representing potential solutions to the problem;

2   applying a fitness function to each genome;

3   building a mating pool by selecting genomes from this population based on their fitness;

4   generating a new population from the mating pool;

5   starting at step 2 again with the new population.

Most of these processes are based on decisions that are made with an element of randomness. The mean fitness of the population is likely to rise as generation succeeds generation.

In the next unit, I am going to look a little more deeply into this whole process, and try to draw out some of the theory that lies behind it.

But before moving on, look back at the learning outcomes for this unit and check these against what you think you can now do. Return to any section of the unit if you feel you need to.

Unit 2: Genetic algorithms

CONTENTS

2 Finding the best strategy

The general problem that GAs set out to solve is finding a global peak in a fitness landscape of unknown shape. The selection operation forces the population to move up any slopes it finds, while crossover and mutation make sure that other places in the solution space are explored. This means that there are two, conflicting, processes taking place: one is the exploration of the solution space, the other is the exploitation of already-found, promising potential solutions. To make the GA efficient, it needs to balance exploration against exploitation. Too much exploration will result in a system that rarely develops promising solutions; conversely, too much exploitation will lead to a system that is likely to be trapped on poor-quality local maxima.

To get a better idea on how to manage this balance between exploration and exploitation, I want to take a slight detour to Las Vegas and examine how to win at the slot machines.

A one-armed bandit (or a slot machine) is a gambling machine. You put money in the slot, pull the lever and drums spin round in the machine. If, when the drums have finished spinning, they show a matching set of symbols, you win a prize. The drum-spinning process is random, and so is the chance of a pay-off but, over a number of trials, you can expect to get an average pay-off of μ pounds (with a standard deviation of σ).

A two-armed bandit (see Figure 2.1) is basically two one-armed bandits stuck together; each machine is entirely independent of the other. (The general case is the k-armed bandit.) Arm 1 gives a pay-off of μ_1 with standard deviation σ_1, and arm 2 gives a pay-off of μ_2 with standard deviation σ_2. If we're given some large amount of cash to play such a machine (so we can carry out a total of N trials), we obviously want to play the arm that will give the highest pay-off. The trouble is, when we start we don't know anything about the pay-off regimes of either arm. What we need to do is to try out both arms for a while and, based on what we learn, make better choices about which arm to use for the next go.

Figure 2.1   A two-armed bandit

One approach is to perform n trials with each arm ($2n < N$), look at the average pay-offs for each arm after those trials, and then play the arm with the highest average for the remaining $N - 2n$ trials. However, there is a chance, which I'll term $q(n)$, that the poorer arm happens to give the better result after these $2n$ trials. This means that we lose out on our maximal winnings in two ways. If the poorer arm pays out the most in our trial, we'll lose $|\mu_1 - \mu_2| \cdot (N - n)$ by playing it after the exploration phase; this happens with probability $q(n)$. If the poorer arm pays out the least, we lose $|\mu_1 - \mu_2| \cdot n$ in the exploration phase; this happens with probability $(1 - q(n))$. We can combine these two factors to give an equation for the amount we can expect to lose against playing the better arm exclusively:

$$L(N,n) = |\mu_1 - \mu_2| \cdot [(N - n) \cdot q(n) + n(1 - q(n))] \tag{2.1}$$

Using this equation (and a suitable description of the probability $q(n)$), we can derive the optimal number of trials we should perform before deciding on which arm to use for the remainder of the time. Holland (1975) derives an expression for the optimal strategy: we should allocate n^* trials to the worse arm and the remaining $N - n^*$ to the better arm, where:

$$n^* = b^2 \ln\left[\frac{N^2}{8\pi b^4 \ln N^2}\right] \quad \text{and} \quad b = \frac{\sigma_1}{(\mu_1 - \mu_2)} \tag{2.2}$$

If we assume that N is large, so that $N - n^* \approx N$, we can rearrange Equation 2.2 to give:

$$N - n^* \approx \sqrt{8\pi b^4 \ln N^2} \cdot e^{n^*/2b^2} \tag{2.3}$$

This means that, as N increases, we should apportion an exponentially increasing number of trials to the better arm. This result gives an upper bound on efficiency, as it presupposes our knowledge of which arm will turn out to be better. The expressions change but the same general result is true for 3-, 4- and more-armed bandits. We should aim towards this ideal of an exponential increase in effort devoted to the most promising results.

How does this apply to GAs? Remember that each individual in a GA has an entire genome and that the fitness of the individual is based on the entire genome. Recall how selection works in biological organisms. The best way to think about the information contained in the genomes is in terms of genes, those sections of a genome that give rise to one particular feature. Understanding evolution is best done in terms of the evolution of genes: each gene contributes to the fitness of the organism and evolution acts so that the genes propagate themselves through the gene pool as effectively as possible. In other words, each gene is playing a k-armed bandit, where each variant of a gene is one of the arms of the bandit, each instance of a gene is one play of the game, and selection for reproduction counts as a pay-off. As the population moves from generation to generation, the total number of trials of each gene, N, increases: N is the number of times each gene could have been tested at any time in the history of the GA's run. As N increases, the optimal number of trials awarded to the best gene should increase exponentially.

As the idea of genes is a powerful one in thinking about evolution in biological organisms, it seems sensible to think about the processing in GAs in the same way. A subset of a genome in a biological organism is called a gene; the subset of a genome in an artificial organism is called a **schema**. In the next section, I'll look at schema theory and what it says about how GAs may work.

Don't worry about where this equation comes from: its derivation requires several pages of dense mathematics. Instead, you just need to understand what this equation says about the allocation of trials.

'Schema' means 'the underlying plan or structure'. Its plural is usually given as 'schemata', though the anglicised 'schemas' is also acceptable.

SAQ 2.1

In the *k*-armed bandit I identified two phases: exploration (where different solutions are discovered) and exploitation (where the best solution is used). These two phases also exist in GAs.

Which of the following operators support(s) exploration and which support(s) exploitation in a GA?

▶ Selection

▶ Crossover

▶ Mutation

ANSWER...

Selection supports exploitation whereas crossover and mutation both support exploration.

3 Schema theory

A schema is a way of identifying some part of a genome, a template if you will. If we take a very simple GA where the genome only consists of binary digits (0 and 1), we need three symbols to represent schemata: 0, 1 and *, where the * means 'don't care'. For instance, ***10**11** is a schema. Schemata need to be the same length as the genomes we're interested in. A schema matches a genome if, for every position, the symbols at the corresponding positions are identical. A ***** in the schema matches any symbol in the genome. For instance, the schema ***100111** matches two strings (**0100111** and **1100111**) while the schema ***100*11** matches four (**0100011**, **0100111**, **1100011** and **1100111**). The schema ***10**11** matches the string **1100111**, but does not match the string **1000111** (the symbols in the second position don't match).

We can extend this idea to genomes made up of more than two symbol types, so long as our schemata have the additional 'don't care' symbol.

SAQ 2.2

How many binary strings are covered by the schema **101**0*1**? List them.

ANSWER..

2^3 = 8 because there are 3 *****s; **10100001**, **10100011**, **10101001**, **10101011**, **10110001**, **10110011**, **10111001**, **10111011**.

SAQ 2.3

Construct a schema for the following list of binary strings:

100000, **100001**, **100010**, **100011**, **101000**, **100001**, **100010**, **100011**, **110000**, **110001**, **110010**, **110011**, **111000**, **111001**, **111010**, **111011**.

ANSWER..
1**0**.

Schemata are generally characterised by two numbers: **order** and **defining length**.

▶ The order of a schema H, written as $o(H)$, is the number of fixed positions in that schema. For instance, the schema ***10**11** is order 4 and ***100111** is order 6. Order is a measure of how specific that schema is; high-order schemata match fewer strings than low-order schemata.

▶ Defining length, written $\delta(H)$, is the distance from the first to the last fixed position in the schema. The schemata ***10**11** and ***100111** both have defining lengths of 5, while the schema ******0**** has a defining length of zero. Schemata with larger defining lengths are more likely to be disrupted by crossover and mutation.

SAQ 2.4

What are the values of $o(H)$ and $\delta(H)$ for the schema H = **101**0*1**?

ANSWER..
H has five fixed positions, so its order, $o(H)$ = 5. The first fixed position is position 1 and the last is position 8, so its defining length, $\delta(H)$ = 7.

The basic idea behind schema theory is that fragments of the genome (the schemata's fixed positions) are responsible for contributions to an individual's overall fitness. A single schema will be tested many times each generation, once for each individual that contains it in the population. Finding the fitness of an individual also contributes to the information about the relative fitness of all the schemata that can make up that individual. The selection step of the GA will generally select those individuals with the highest fitness and therefore those schemata that most contribute to that fitness will be more commonly represented.

For instance, consider the task of trying to find a genome that encodes for the largest binary number. Let's take the number that a genome encodes as its fitness. If we have a small population of six individuals, as shown in Table 2.1, we can see that individuals with the **1******* schema have an average fitness of 45.7, while individuals with the **0******* schema have an average fitness of 20.3. Similarly, the schema *******1** has a fitness of 31 and *******0** has a fitness of 34. There is a clear difference in fitness between **1******* and **0******, but *******1** and *******0** have very similar fitnesses. Any sensible GA will be more likely to select the fittest individuals, so we can expect that the next generation will have more instances of **1******* than **0******, but there will be little pressure to select *******1** over *******0**, so the proportions of these schemata in the next generation will be more open.

Table 2.1

Individual	Fitness
001101	13
100110	38
011010	26
110010	50
110001	49
010110	22

Now we understand what's going on, we can express the ideas more formally and derive some quantitative results. We start with a collection of individuals, A_1, A_2 ... A_n, contained in the population $\mathbf{A}(t)$ at generation t. In that population, there will be $m(H,t)$ individuals with a particular schema H. During reproduction, an individual is selected with a probability p_i based on its fitness f_i:

$$p_i = \frac{f_i}{\sum f_j} ,$$

where j ranges over 1 to n. If we pick (with replacement) a population of size n from $\mathbf{A}(t)$, we will have:

$$E[m(H,t+1)] = m(H,t) \cdot n \cdot \frac{f(H)}{\sum f_j} \tag{2.4}$$

where $E(x)$ is the expected value of x and $f(H)$ is the average fitness of all individuals that represent the schema H. The average fitness of the population can be written as:

$$\bar{f} = \frac{\sum f_j}{n}$$

so we can rewrite Equation 2.4 as:

$$E[m(H,t+1)] = m(H,t)\frac{f(H)}{\bar{f}} \tag{2.5}$$

This means that we expect the number of examples of a schema to grow in proportion to the fitness it contributes to individuals that contain it. Schemata with above-average fitness will be more represented and those with below-average fitness will be less represented. This is carried out in parallel for all schemata in the population.

If we assume that a particular schema H is always above average by a factor c, we can write $f(H) = \overline{f} + c\overline{f}$ and rewrite Equation 2.5 as:

$$E[m(H,t+1)] = m(H,t)\frac{\overline{f} + c\overline{f}}{\overline{f}} = m(H,t) \cdot (1+c) \tag{2.6}$$

Starting with $m(H,0)$, we can write $E[m(H,1)] = m(H,0) \cdot (1 + c)$, $E[m(H,2)] = m(H,0) \cdot (1 + c) \cdot (1 + c) = m(H,0) \cdot (1 + c)^2$, and so on. In general:

$$E[m(H,t)] = m(H,0) \cdot (1+c)^t \tag{2.7}$$

which is the equation for calculating compound interest and has an exponential solution. This means that, as the GA progresses from generation to generation, the fittest schemata are represented by an exponentially increasing number of individuals and the least fit schemata are represented by an exponentially decaying number of individuals. You may recall from our discussion of the k-armed bandit in Section 2 that the optimal strategy for playing a k-armed bandit is to allocate an exponentially increasing number of trials to the observed best arm. As each instance of a given schema counts as a trial, and the best schemata are represented by an exponentially increasing number of individuals, we can see that using schema theory gives us a lens to see that a GA seems to follow a near-optimal strategy to find the highest-fitness schemata: when those schemata are combined into a single individual, it will have found the optimal solution to the problem.

Equation 2.5 may lead to this encouraging result, but it doesn't reflect the reality of what happens in a GA very well because the operations of crossover and mutation will also act to create or destroy schemata. However, we can include the effects of these operators to give a more accurate expression for the expected number of instances of a particular schema. I'll start by looking at the effects of crossover. To keep things simple, I'll only consider the destructive effects of these two operations, so we'll get a lower bound on the prevalence of a schema in our population.

3.1 Crossover

Single-point crossover occurs by splitting the genome at a single, randomly chosen point and swapping the former sections. If the crossover point happens to lie within the defining length of a schema, that schema will be destroyed (unless the other parent happens to be identical at the schema's fixed positions, a possibility we'll ignore as we're after the worst-case solution). For instance, consider the genome **0101011** and two of the schemata contained in it: schema H_1 is ***10***1** and schema H_2 is ****010****. As these genomes are seven bits long, there are six sites where crossover could occur. There is only one crossover site (after position 1) that will preserve H_1; crossover at any other site will destroy it.

SAQ 2.5

At how many sites can crossover occur so that H_2 is preserved?

ANSWER...

There are four sites for crossover that will preserve H_2: after positions 1, 2, 5 and 6.

This means that, if crossover occurs, there is a 5/6 chance that H_1 will be destroyed, but only a 2/6 chance that H_2 will be destroyed. The probability is controlled by the defining length of the schema compared to the length of the genome: shorter schemata are more likely to survive crossover. We can write the chance of survival of a schema under crossover ($S_c(H)$) as being:

$$S_c(H) \geq 1 - p_c \frac{\delta(H)}{l-1} \tag{2.8}$$

where p_c is the probability of crossover occurring and l is the length of the genome.

SAQ 2.6

Why is Equation 2.8 an inequality, not an equality?

ANSWER...

The reason is that, as stated previously, some crossover operations will preserve a schema even if the crossover site is within the schema. This occurs if both parents have the same elements at the schema's fixed positions.

3.2 Mutation

We can look at the destructive effects of mutation in a similar way. Each element of a schema has a mutation probability of p_m. A schema will only survive if no element is mutated, which depends on the order of the schema. The chance of survival of a schema under mutation ($S_m(H)$) is:

$$S_m(H) = (1 - p_m)^{o(H)} \tag{2.9}$$

These two results allow us to modify Equation 2.5 to include crossover and mutation:

$$E\left[m(H,t+1)\right] \geq m(H,t) \frac{f(H)}{\bar{f}} \cdot \left(1 - p_c \frac{\delta(H)}{l-1}\right) \cdot (1 - p_m)^{o(H)} \tag{2.10}$$

Equation 2.10 is known as the **schema theorem** and is a fundamental result of schema theory. It shows how GAs favour the growth of schemata with high relative fitness and low defining lengths. Such schemata are known as **building blocks**. I'll talk more about building blocks below.

Given that we're talking about GAs in terms of schemata instead of individuals, it would be nice to know how many schemata there are in the population and how many of them are usefully processed in a GA.

A given population will have representatives of many more schemata than there are individuals. For instance, the string 11010 is a representative of 2^5 schemata (as each position in the string may take on its actual value or the 'don't care' symbol. In a given population of n individuals, each with a genome of length l, there will be between 2^l and $n2^l$ different schemata. Consideration of which schemata appear in the population leads to the result that a population of n individuals will process something proportional to n^3 different schemata. This ability of GAs to process many more schemata than would be apparent at first glance is termed **implicit parallelism** and is touted as the main reason why GAs are so successful at finding optimal or near-optimal solutions.

A good way to increase the number of schemata in a population is to increase the length of the genomes. The way to do this, while ensuring that every position in the genome is meaningful, is to reduce the number of letters in the alphabet used to build the genome. The ultimate endpoint of this is to have a genome made up of only two letters. This is one reason why much GA research uses binary genome alphabets. This consideration has become known as the 'principle of minimal alphabets'.

3.3 Royal Roads and deception

Schema theory says that GAs work though the selection and combination of building blocks. Building blocks are schemata with short defining lengths that confer high fitness on the individual of which they are part. For instance, if we have a genome that consists of binary digits, whose fitness is evaluated by interpreting the genome as a binary number, the schema **11****** will be considered a building block. It also suggests that these building blocks are cumulative: if an individual has two or more building blocks, its fitness will be higher than if it only had one. These predictions have been tested, and the results were somewhat surprising.

Royal Road functions are a class of fitness functions that are meant to capture the essence of building blocks in an idealised form. The evaluation function for the Royal Road experiment was based on a 64-bit genome. The genome had eight schema templates (see Figure 2.2); the fitness of a genome is found by summing the coefficients c_i for each schema x_i that matches it. The expectation is that each of the eight building blocks would be found by a different individual and that crossover would bring the building blocks together.

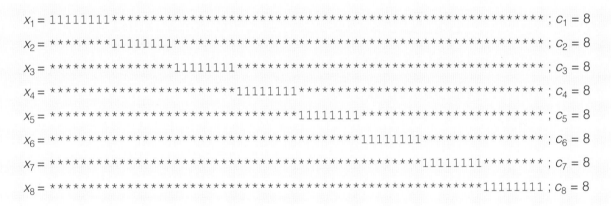

$$x_1 = 11111111** \; ; \; c_1 = 8$$
$$x_2 = ********11111111** \; ; \; c_2 = 8$$
$$x_3 = ****************11111111************************************ \; ; \; c_3 = 8$$
$$x_4 = ************************11111111**************************** \; ; \; c_4 = 8$$
$$x_5 = ********************************11111111******************** \; ; \; c_5 = 8$$
$$x_6 = **11111111************ \; ; \; c_6 = 8$$
$$x_7 = **11111111******** \; ; \; c_7 = 8$$
$$x_8 = **11111111 \; ; \; c_8 = 8$$

Figure 2.2   The Royal Road fitness function. c_n represents the partial fitness of schema x_n

To see how GAs performed, a standard GA was pitted against a number of hill-climbing algorithms that started with a random individual, flipped some bits in the genome and checked to see if any single bit-flip resulted in an increase in fitness. One particular function (choosing a random bit to flip and rejecting the change only if it reduced the individual's fitness) found the optimal genome around ten times more quickly than the GA!

Hill-climbing was briefly discussed in Unit 2 of Block 2.

Computer Exercise 2.1

Now do Computer Exercise 2.1 on the course DVD, where you will explore the Royal Roads Problem.

The reason for this is that the various schemata interact in the population and successfully finding one good schema can hamper attempts to find others, an effect termed **hitchhiking**. If one schema (x_3, say) is found early in the GA's run, that schema will spread quickly through the population. As that schema spreads, the other bits in the genome with this schema will also be spread throughout the population. These other bits will include lots of zeros and they will be associated with the high fitness of the found schema. The presence, and propagation, of these zeros will tend to eliminate any chance discoveries of other, nearby schemata. In other words, a GA does not take independent samples throughout the space of possible genomes and this hampers the GA in its search for the optimal solution.

SAQ 2.7

Why does hitchhiking tend to suppress schemata with similar sets of fixed positions, not those that are more different?

ANSWER...

Because crossover tends to keep contiguous sections of the genome together. Zeros near a found schema are unlikely to be removed by crossover, while zeros further away are more likely to be exchanged.

The Royal Roads Problem is just one example of a problem that is difficult for GAs to solve. Researchers looked around for reasons why GAs seemed to fail (i.e. take a long time to solve, if they solved it at all) on several problems while succeeding on other, very similar problems. The notion of **deception** arose to explain this.

A deceptive problem is one where the best building blocks (short, fit schemata) come together to form a sub-optimal solution. We can see this by looking at, for example, the average fitnesses of the different schemata in the problem shown in Table 2.2. The average fitness of the **11*** schema is $(4 + 5) \div 2 = 4.5$.

Table 2.2   A deceptive problem

Genome	Fitness
000	6
001	1
010	1
011	4
100	1
101	4
110	4
111	5

Exercise 2.1

Calculate the average fitnesses of the **00***, **1**** and **0**** schemata.

Answer..

The fitnesses are:

00*: $(6 + 1) \div 2 = 3.5$

1**: $(1 + 4 + 4 + 5) \div 4 = 3.5$

0**: $(6 + 1 + 1 + 4) \div 4 = 3$

Both the **1**** and **11*** schemata have higher average fitnesses than their competitors (**0**** and **00*** respectively), so the schema theorem suggests that these apparently best building blocks should be propagated so that they dominate the population. This would lead to a situation where the GA cannot find the optimal solution because all its building blocks have been cleansed from the population. Unfortunately, this insight doesn't seem to be that useful in practice, for many 'deceptive' problems can be solved by real GAs, and many deceptive problems can be made non-deceptive by rescaling the fitness function.

3.4 Shortcomings of schema theory

As we've seen, schema theory and the building block hypothesis are intuitively appealing. The trouble is, they don't work very well in explaining how GAs work, and they're not very good at allowing us to make predictions about how GAs will operate. This suggests that there are some flaws in schema theory. Taking a critical look at schema theory will show us where some of these flaws may lie.

Exercise 2.2

Look again at the derivation of Equation 2.7, which shows that the most favourable schemata will appear in an exponentially increasing number of individuals. What assumptions were made in the derivation of this equation?

Answer..

We made four assumptions, some explicit and some implicit:

1   Above-average schema will exponentially increase in number, even in a finite population.

2   A fit schema will always be a constant factor more fit than the population as a whole.

3   The number of instances of a schema that actually appear in a generation is the same as the number of instances of that schema that we expect to appear from looking at the generation before.

4   The values of 'don't care' positions in the schema are evenly distributed so that competing schemata can be fairly compared.

Don't worry if you didn't get all of these: some of the points are quite subtle.

As should be obvious, none of these need be true in practice. Indeed, assumptions 1 and 2 will always be false in any real GA. If any schema receives an exponentially increasing number of trials, it will take only a few generations for that schema to be required to appear more often than there are individuals in the population. The best that we can hope for is that the schema will have an increasing number of trials in the initial stages of a GA's run, but in practice the population curve of even the best schema will be something like a sigmoid curve. As regards assumption 2, the average fitness of the population will tend to increase with each generation. If a fit schema is represented more frequently with each generation, its fitness advantage will be eroded over time as the rest of the population becomes more fit (perhaps by containing more copies of the schema under consideration). Consideration of these two assumptions indicates that the schema theorem will only be true in the early stages of a GA's run.

You were introduced to the sigmoid function in Block 4.

But things are worse than that. The schema theorem can only be applied to predict the outcome of one generation from the previous, and not to predict what will happen in several generations' time. Equations 2.6 and 2.10 give values for the expected number of instances of a schema in generation $n + 1$ given information about generation n. The *actual* number of copies of a schema is completely open, as all the operations (selection, crossover, and mutation) are stochastic. The expected value given by Equations 2.6 and 2.10 will only be the actual value in the limit of an infinite population. For any finite population, the best we can do is to give confidence intervals on the range of number of schema instances; we cannot give a definite answer to the outcome of a stochastic process.

Knowing that we have a finite population adds a further complication to the basis of the schema theorem. The whole edifice of schema theory relies on the foundation that competing schemata can be judged fairly by looking at the average fitness of individuals that contain those schemata. This requires that the values of the 'don't care' positions are distributed evenly, and that the distribution of the 'don't care' positions are similar between all the competing schemata under consideration. Given a finite population, this may very well not be the case. It could be that most of the instances of the schema **1***** are also instances of **1*0*** while most instances of **0***** are also instances of **0*1***. In this case, there is nothing we can say about the relative fitness of the competing order-1 schemata **1***** and **0***** as there is no analysis we can do that is independent of the order-2 schemata. In this case, we're not actually selecting between the order-1 schemata at all and the basis of schema theory disappears.

Finally, there are some other considerations that have come from other research looking at the reliability of schema theory. It turns out that while exponentially increasing trials form an upper bound on the optimal strategy for playing a k-armed bandit, there are other approaches that are better. Other research has also suggested that the notion of what a schema is needs to be rethought for non-binary alphabets: a single 'don't care' element isn't sufficient, but instead we need to specify exactly which alternatives could replace the 'don't care' elements and consider each sets of alternatives independently.

Schema theory has long been touted as an intellectual framework for GAs. However, this brief critique of it has shown that schema theory isn't a good theory in terms of the desiderata given at the start of this unit: it doesn't predict performance, it doesn't suggest values for various parameters, and it doesn't even say whether a given problem is easily soluble. But what alternatives to schema theory, if any, are there?

In the next two sections, I'll look at two alternative and contrasting approaches to explaining why GAs work. First, I'll look at an approach that focuses on the individuals in a GA's population and tries to characterise precisely the behaviour of those individuals. Then, I'll look at ways of modelling the population as a whole by ignoring most distinctions between individuals.

4 Markov processes

Every process in a GA (selection, mutation and crossover) is stochastic: the result of applying these operators results in a random outcome. Many other processes in the world are stochastic: games of chance and radioactive decay are genuinely stochastic; sequences such as blood pressure readings and the generation of words in a sentence are examples of processes that can usefully be thought of as stochastic. If we want to develop a theory of GAs, perhaps a good place to start would be with the theory of stochastic processes.

In the simplest case (sufficient for our purposes), a stochastic process is a sequence of discrete, random events occurring at discrete points in time. Each event determines the state of the system. The set of events (and states) is finite. For a GA, the event could be the genome of an individual (bounded by the possible states of the genome) with the times given by the generation number. As the next state is chosen randomly, we can write down the probability distribution over the set of states that gives the likelihood of each state occurring next. For simple stochastic processes such as rolling a die, the value of the next state is independent of the current state, but for more complex ones (such as GAs) the probability distribution for the next state depends on the current state.

SAQ 2.8

Write down the probability distribution for rolling a fair, six-sided die.

ANSWER...
The probability of rolling each number is the same, as shown in Table 2.3.

Table 2.3

Event	Probability
1	1/6
2	1/6
3	1/6
4	1/6
5	1/6
6	1/6

One important class of stochastic processes is when the probability distribution of the next state depends purely on the current state: what happens next is independent of the history of the system. This property is called the **Markov property** and a process with the Markov property is called a **Markov process**. The sequence of states through which a Markov process goes is called a **Markov chain**. For any Markov process, we can write down a probability distribution for each state that gives the probability of each state occurring next. If we label each possible state with a number, starting with one, we can write down the probability distribution for what happens after state i as:

$$p(s_1 \mid s_i) = p_{1i}$$
$$p(s_2 \mid s_i) = p_{2i}$$
$$p(s_3 \mid s_i) = p_{3i}$$

and so on. It could be that some probabilities are zero, and it's likely that the probability distribution given by each state will be different. As we can enumerate all the states, we can completely describe the system by writing down such a probability distribution for each state. In this case, it's notationally easier to describe the system with a matrix of these conditional probabilities:

$$\mathbf{P} = \begin{bmatrix} p_{11} & p_{12} & \cdots & p_{1n} \\ p_{21} & p_{22} & \cdots & p_{2n} \\ \vdots & \vdots & \ddots & \vdots \\ p_{n1} & p_{n2} & \cdots & p_{nn} \end{bmatrix} = \begin{bmatrix} p(s_1 \mid s_1) & p(s_1 \mid s_2) & \cdots & p(s_1 \mid s_n) \\ p(s_2 \mid s_1) & p(s_2 \mid s_2) & \cdots & p(s_2 \mid s_n) \\ \vdots & \vdots & \ddots & \vdots \\ p(s_n \mid s_1) & p(s_n \mid s_2) & \cdots & p(s_n \mid s_n) \end{bmatrix} \quad (2.11)$$

where each p_{ij} is the probability of state i coming after state j. Such a matrix is called a **transition matrix**. If we express the state of an individual with the column vector:

$$\mathbf{s}_0 = \begin{bmatrix} 0 \\ \vdots \\ 1 \\ \vdots \\ 0 \end{bmatrix}$$

where the sole 1 is in the row corresponding to this state, we can calculate the probabilities of the next state with the equation:

$$\mathbf{s}_1 = \mathbf{P} \cdot \mathbf{s}_0 \quad (2.12)$$

Now that we've seen that Markov processes can be used to model GAs, it's time to look at what the theory would give us. Basically, using the theory of Markov processes can tell us a lot about the long-term trends of a system. It can tell us how a system moves from state to state; it can tell us what the long-term steady state looks like; it can even tell us if a long-term steady state exists.

To make the discussion a bit more concrete, I'll look at a simple example involving soap brands. Let's imagine that the Acme Soap Company is launching SupaSoap, a new brand of hand soap. It wants to know how its soap will fare against its main rival, LatherPlus (which has a market share of 23%), and against other brands and generic soaps. Acme has done some market research and focus group testing and has come up with the set of probabilities for brand loyalty and brand switching given in Table 2.4.

Table 2.4

Brand to:	Brand from:		
	SupaSoap	LatherPlus	Other
SupaSoap	28%	1%	16%
LatherPlus	4%	25%	15%
Other	68%	74%	69%

For example, if a person bought LatherPlus last month, there is a 1% chance that they'll buy SupaSoap this month, a 25% chance that they'll buy LatherPlus again, and a 74% chance they'll buy some other brand. Acme can use this information to predict the probability, over subsequent months, that someone who initially buys LatherPlus will end up buying SupaSoap. But it can also use the same process to understand how many of a group of people, each making their own, independent decisions, will end up buying SupaSoap. Indeed, it can look at an arbitrarily large group of shoppers by making $\mathbf{s}_0$ in Equation 2.12 equal to the initial distribution of buying behaviour:

$$\mathbf{s}_1 = \mathbf{P} \cdot \mathbf{s}_0 = \begin{bmatrix} 0.28 & 0.01 & 0.16 \\ 0.04 & 0.25 & 0.15 \\ 0.68 & 0.74 & 0.69 \end{bmatrix} \cdot \begin{bmatrix} 0 \\ 0.23 \\ 0.77 \end{bmatrix} = \begin{bmatrix} 0.126 \\ 0.173 \\ 0.701 \end{bmatrix}$$

$$\mathbf{s}_2 = \mathbf{P} \cdot \mathbf{s}_1 = \begin{bmatrix} 0.28 & 0.01 & 0.16 \\ 0.04 & 0.25 & 0.15 \\ 0.68 & 0.74 & 0.69 \end{bmatrix} \cdot \begin{bmatrix} 0.126 \\ 0.173 \\ 0.701 \end{bmatrix} = \begin{bmatrix} 0.149 \\ 0.154 \\ 0.697 \end{bmatrix}$$

$$\mathbf{s}_3 = \mathbf{P} \cdot \mathbf{s}_2 = \begin{bmatrix} 0.28 & 0.01 & 0.16 \\ 0.04 & 0.25 & 0.15 \\ 0.68 & 0.74 & 0.69 \end{bmatrix} \cdot \begin{bmatrix} 0.149 \\ 0.154 \\ 0.697 \end{bmatrix} = \begin{bmatrix} 0.155 \\ 0.149 \\ 0.696 \end{bmatrix}$$

As you can see, the market share of SupaSoap goes from 0% to 13% to 15% to 16%. After three months, SupaSoap has overtaken LatherPlus, the market leader. You can also see that, while SupaSoap continues to gain market share, the rate at which it does so is decreasing. This implies that there is an equilibrium value for the Markov process, where the market shares are equal. At the equilibrium, $\mathbf{s}_{n+1} = \mathbf{P} \cdot \mathbf{s}_n = \mathbf{s}_n$. This can be solved and the equilibrium distribution found: for the soap example, the eventual steady state has SupaSoap with 15.7% of the market, LatherPlus with 14.8% and other brands taking 69.5%.

More interesting results come from Markov process theory when there are some zeros and ones in the transition matrix. In this case, some states are not reachable from others. The states could be reachable indirectly, the states could form two (or more) distinct and non-communicating subsets, or there could be **absorbing states**. Absorbing states are interesting because, if a system enters such a state, it can never leave it. An absorbing state can be identified because its column in the transition matrix is all zeros except for a single entry of 1 on the main diagonal. If it is possible to move to an absorbing state, it is obvious that the long-term behaviour of the system is to move to that absorbing state and stay there: given enough time, the system will randomly move to an absorbing state and then be unable to move to another state. A system may have more than one absorbing state, in which case an analysis of the transition matrix and the starting distribution can determine the likelihood of any of the absorbing states being reached. An example of an absorbing state in the GA example is an individual with satisficing fitness (i.e. one that satisfies only the minimum requirements necessary to achieve its goal).

We've seen that Markov process theory can model the evolution of stochastic systems, such as we see in GAs. Now we need to look at how to represent a GA in these terms. The obvious representation is the one described above: enumerate all the states of a genome and develop the transition matrix for how an individual changes over time. The problem with this approach is that it is still too low level a description of the state of a GA process. What we're really interested in is the state of the population as a whole in each generation.

As the genome is finite, we can enumerate all the possible states of the genome. Given that the population is also finite, we can enumerate all the possible states of the population: for instance, one state would be when all the individuals have genome type 1, another would be when all but one individual is of type 1 while the remaining one is of type 2, and so on. We can now start to look at how to develop the transition matrix for the population, to show how it will change from one population to another as the GA operates.

First, let's consider the effects of selection alone. This will not create any new types of individual in the population, but is likely to change the proportions of those individuals.

SAQ 2.9

What is special about populations that contain only one type of individual?

ANSWER..

These are absorbing states. If a population is homogeneous, the creation of a new population by selection only can only create another homogeneous population.

Things get more interesting when we consider the effects of mutation. Mutation is capable of changing any individual into any other type of individual. The probability of a large change in the genome is small, but it is non-zero. As this is true for all individuals in a population, the overall effect of mutation is to allow any population to mutate into any other population in a single generation: every entry in the transition matrix will be non-zero, so there are no absorbing states. This means that, while there will be a steady-state probability distribution over populations, all populations will be possible and the Markov process will visit all of them eventually and repeatedly, given enough time.

Including crossover in the GA doesn't make any difference to this conclusion. Crossover is just another way of rearranging the genomes in the population, and the action of mutation is sufficient to allow the GA to move from any population state to any other with a non-zero probability.

However, having our optimisation process visit every possible state, without halting on any good ones, is somewhat less than desirable. What we want is an optimisation process that will, over time, converge on the optimal solution: as the process moves forward, it gets closer and closer to the optimum and never undoes the progress it makes. What we want from our optimising GA is some way of ensuring that we don't lose the best individuals in our population. We've already seen that this won't happen with any stochastic method of selection and mutation, so we need to include some non-stochastic element in our GA. How can we do this?

Exercise 2.3

Suppose you're rolling a pair of dice but the score of a roll is the value of the highest die. How can you ensure that your score never decreases?

Answer...

Initially, roll both dice. After that, only ever roll the die showing the lowest value. If you get a tie, choose one randomly.

As this exercise shows, we can make a stochastic process converge on an optimal value if we include a non-stochastic element. For a GA, the easiest way to do this is by modifying the selection operation. One standard approach is termed **elitism** and it's what I suggested in Exercise 2.3. In each generation, we remember the best individual we've found (call it *b*). If, in the next generation, there is not an individual that's at least as good as *b*, we replace a random member of the new generation with *b*.

This ensures that the best individual in a population never gets worse from generation to generation and that the GA will eventually converge on the optimal solution. (More formally, the probability that the optimal solution will not be found diminishes to zero as the number of generations goes to infinity.)

A general consideration of GAs from the perspective of Markov processes has allowed us to prove that elitism is necessary for a GA to converge. But there is one large difficulty with looking at specific instances of how GAs solve problems: the vast size of the transition matrices involved. If we have a mere fifty individuals in a population, each containing a genome of fifty bits (giving rise to 2^{50} distinct types of individual), there are some 10^{688} distinct populations that could exist. To model this as a Markov process, we would have to generate a transition matrix with 10^{1376} elements. This qualifies to be called 'unfeasibly large'. There has been some work done on reducing the size of the transition matrices needed by combining states that are to some extent similar. Despite this work, it seems that the overall approach is doomed to failure.

However, there are simplifications that can be made if we assume that the population is infinite in size, in which case the analysis becomes similar to that of linear programming optimisation methods, the details of which are beyond the scope of this course.

5 Statistical mechanics

Let's take a moment to reflect on how GAs operate. They involve a population of essentially indistinguishable individuals, each characterised by a few state variables (the genome and fitness). Operations such as selection and mutation operate at the level of these individuals. However, as users of GAs, we're not concerned with the precise state of every individual in the population. Instead, we're interested in the population as a whole and its statistics, such as the average fitness and diversity. In other words, we're interested in how the processes at the microscopic scale give rise to the macroscopic behaviour of the population as a whole. If the population is large, we can take averages over all the populations and use these as the macroscopic quantities.

This is a state of affairs that is very familiar to physicists who study the bulk properties of matter such as gases. In a gas, each molecule has its one-state variables (position and momentum) and reacts to purely microscopic forces (such as collisions with other molecules). However, in most cases, physicists are interested in macroscopic properties such as the pressure of the gas and the range of momenta of molecules in the gas. The study of how these microscopic events give rise to macroscopic properties is termed statistical mechanics. Given the similarities between the subject of this branch of physics and GAs, it seems reasonable to see how far statistical mechanics can be applied to the study of GAs.

Statistical mechanics is not concerned with the fate of individuals; rather, it is concerned with populations as a whole and how those populations change over time as a GA operates. Most work using statistical mechanics concentrates on the distribution of fitness among the population (see Figure 2.3). The aim of the statistical mechanics approach is to predict how this fitness distribution changes over time. For this to happen, we need to characterise the distribution of fitness values in the population. This is done through a series of values called **cumulants**.

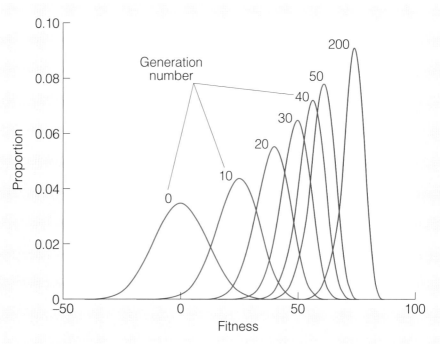

Figure 2.3 Fitness distribution changing over time. Each curve is labelled with the generation number. In early generations, the distribution has a low mean and large variance, and then, as the generation number increases, the mean increases and the variance decreases

The first cumulant of a distribution is its mean and the second is its variance. These should be familiar to you. Figures 2.4(a) and 2.4(b) show distributions with different values of these cumulants. Figure 2.4(a) shows how changing the mean moves the entire curve along the x-axis without changing its shape, while Figure 2.4(b) shows how increasing the variance flattens and broadens the curve. The third cumulant is the skew of the distribution and shows how asymmetrical the distribution is; Figure 2.4(c) shows how decreasing the skew moves the peak of the curve towards the right, giving an asymmetric curve. The fourth cumulant is kurtosis, a measure of the 'spikiness' of the distribution; Figure 2.4(d) shows how increasing the kurtosis gives a sharper, higher peak but with higher values for the long tails. There are an infinite number of higher cumulants and together they exactly specify the shape of any distribution.

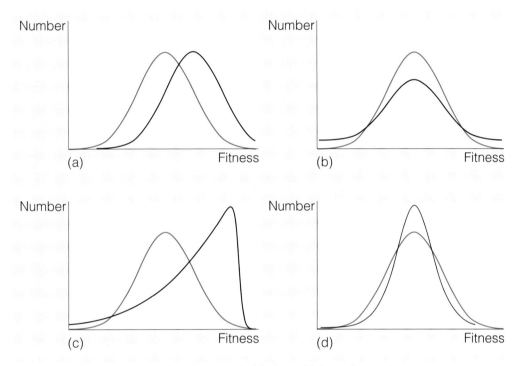

Figure 2.4   Changing (a) mean. (b) variance. (c) skew. (d) kurtosis

We now seem to have swapped a hard problem for an impossible one: instead of tracking a large (but finite) number of individuals, we have to track an infinite number of cumulants. Luckily, in practice, most of these cumulants will have very low values. A normal (Gaussian) distribution is exactly described by the first two cumulants alone, with all others being zero. Any distribution which approximates a normal distribution will have small values for the higher cumulants, and the values of the higher cumulants will become progressively smaller. As you can see from Figure 2.3, most distributions of fitness values found in GA runs are approximately normal. This means that we can approximate the shape of the fitness distribution with only a few cumulants.

The mathematics of deriving expressions for cumulants is quite hairy, and I won't go into it here. However, by considering the effects of selection, mutation, crossover, and the constraint that the range of fitness values is finite, we can derive expressions for the cumulants of later generations in terms of cumulants of earlier ones. For instance, if we take the very simplified problem of generating a new population purely by roulette-wheel selection, ignoring crossover and mutation, and assuming an

You looked briefly at roulette-wheel selection in Unit 1 of this block.

infinite range of fitnesses, we can write the following expressions for the first three cumulants:

$$\kappa_1\big(F(\mathbf{p})\big) = \kappa_1(\mathbf{p}) + \left(\frac{\kappa_2(\mathbf{p})}{\kappa_1(\mathbf{p})}\right)$$

$$\kappa_2\big(F(\mathbf{p})\big) = \kappa_2(\mathbf{p}) - \left(\frac{\kappa_2(\mathbf{p})}{\kappa_1(\mathbf{p})}\right)^2 + \left(\frac{\kappa_3(\mathbf{p})}{\kappa_1(\mathbf{p})}\right)$$

$$\kappa_3\big(F(\mathbf{p})\big) = \kappa_3(\mathbf{p}) + \left(\frac{\kappa_2(\mathbf{p})}{\kappa_1(\mathbf{p})}\right)^3 - \left(\frac{3\kappa_2(\mathbf{p})\kappa_3(\mathbf{p})}{\kappa_1(\mathbf{p})}\right) + \left(\frac{\kappa_4(\mathbf{p})}{\kappa_1(\mathbf{p})}\right)$$

(2.13)

where $\kappa_n(\mathbf{p})$ is the nth cumulant of the population $\mathbf{p}$, and $F(\mathbf{p})$ is the population that arises from $\mathbf{p}$ after selection. Inspection of these equations yields some insight into how the population will evolve. We can see that the mean, $\kappa_1(\mathbf{p})$, will increase and the variance, $\kappa_2(\mathbf{p})$, will decrease. The equation for $\kappa_3(\mathbf{p})$ shows that the skew will increase rapidly. This corresponds with our intuition that selection alone will cause the population to converge on the few high-fitness members of the initial population (see Figure 2.5).

> Our initial population is likely to have a normal fitness distribution, so $\kappa_3(\mathbf{p})$ and $\kappa_4(\mathbf{p})$ will be small.

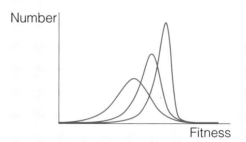

Figure 2.5   Changes in a population's fitness distribution under selection only

We can also include factors for crossover, mutation and the effects of a limited fitness scale and a finite population size. When modelling the first two situations, we need to know how crossover and mutation affect the fitness of an individual. If we assume a simple *unitation* fitness function (the fitness is given by the number of 1s in the binary genome), we see that crossover won't affect the average fitness, so the behaviour of the mean and variance, $\kappa_1(\mathbf{p})$ and $\kappa_2(\mathbf{p})$ respectively, is given by:

$$\kappa_1\big(C \circ U \circ F(\mathbf{p})\big) = ul + (1 - 2u)\left(\kappa_1(\mathbf{p}) + \frac{\kappa_2(\mathbf{p})}{\kappa_1(\mathbf{p})}\right)$$

$$\kappa_2\big(C \circ U \circ F(\mathbf{p})\big) = \kappa_1\big(C \circ U \circ F(\mathbf{p})\big)\left(1 - \frac{\kappa_1\big(C \circ U \circ F(\mathbf{p})\big)}{l}\right)$$

(2.14)

where l is the length of the genome, u is the probability of mutation, and $C \circ U \circ F(\mathbf{p})$ shows the composition of selection, mutation and crossover.

Exercise 2.4

Spend the next few minutes thinking about why crossover won't affect the average fitness of a population when we use the *unitation* fitness function. Write down your answer.

Answer...

Crossover neither creates nor destroys 1s, it merely moves them from place to place. Individuals may change in fitness quite dramatically, but the average will remain the same.

We can substitute the expression for κ_2 into the first expression in Equation 2.14 and solve the recurrence relation that results, to give a value for the fix-point of κ_1, the value of κ_1 as time tends to infinity:

$$\kappa_1 = \frac{l(ul + 1 - 2u)}{2ul + 1 - 2u} \tag{2.15}$$

This is plotted in Figure 2.6, which shows that increasing the mutation rate decreases the final average fitness. This is to be expected, as a high mutation rate will tend to destroy high-fitness genomes.

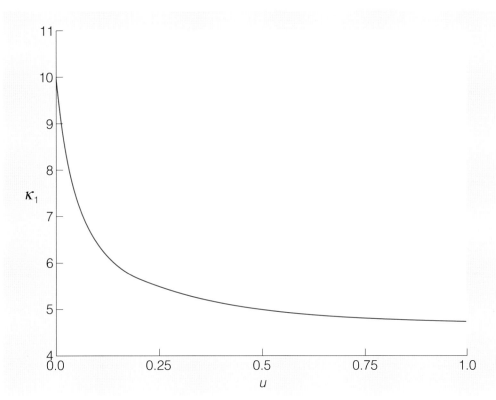

Figure 2.6   Graph of Equation 2.15 for $l = 10$

You should note, however, that Equations 2.14 and 2.15 are only valid for solving the *unitation* problem and under some additional simplifying assumptions about crossover. If you want to apply this approach to any other problem, you have to consider the effects of mutation and crossover on your problem and re-derive Equation 2.14 under that consideration. This is not always easy.

The results from the statistical mechanics analysis are important because they make predictions about future fitness distributions, which are validated by experiment. This approach also links the parameters used in a GA run (fitness function, mutation rate, genome length) to the expected macroscopic behaviours. This means that we can use this approach to predict the optimal values of these parameters for use in a GA. The downside is that we need a good understanding of the problem space in order to derive expressions for the various cumulants, and that isn't always possible for the interesting, and hence difficult, problems we want to solve.

6 No Free Lunch theorem

Just when you might have thought we were getting somewhere with the analysis of GAs, I've got some bad news to share with you. In computer-based optimisation, as in life, there is no such thing as a free lunch. The trouble is, 'No Free Lunch' (or NFL) is a proven theorem in computer science and it states that no optimisation algorithm can ever do better than random chance, when averaged over all possible problems.

6.1 Proof that there's No Free Lunch

The proof of NFL is fairly simple. Optimisation problems can all be thought of as having an optimisation strategy (such as a simple GA), a problem being worked on (such as a particular instance of the TSP) and a pay-off that describes how well that strategy works on that problem. We can express the relationship between these three in the form $y = f(x)$, where x is the strategy, f is the problem and y is the pay-off. The strategies can be anything: GAs, neural nets, symbolic machine learning, random search, divining the next move from examining the cracks on the shoulder blade of a lamb that's been flung into a fire, anything. So long as it is a process by which we can generate decisions, it's classed as a strategy.

Because we're working with finite digital computers, we're only interested in strategies, problems and pay-offs that can be expressed in finite and discrete terms. In other words, we could (in principle) enumerate all possible computer-based optimisation strategies, just as it's possible to enumerate all possible computer programs. This means that we can create a pay-off matrix that relates these three items together.

First, we need to see how large this matrix is. Let's call X the set of all possible optimisation strategies, Y the set of all possible pay-offs, and F the set of all possible problems. Given that each $f \in F$ maps one particular $x \in X$ to a specific $y \in Y$, we can determine the size of F. If $|X| = 1$, there can be no more than $|Y|$ distinct problems. If $|X| = 2$, there can be no more than $|Y|^2$ distinct problems. In general, there are at most $|Y|^{|X|}$ distinct mappings from X to Y, and this is the maximal size of F: $|F| = |Y|^{|X|}$.

Given the limit on the size of F, we can now draw up our matrix connecting xs, ys and fs. Let's call it the **fundamental matrix**. The matrix will have one row for each distinct x and one column for each distinct f. Each element in the matrix will be the performance of that strategy on that problem, the relevant y value. I'll assume that the pay-off is the index of the element of Y but, as we'll see, how we arrange the pay-offs doesn't matter. Of course, this matrix is far too large to actually write, but in principle we could do it, and do it in a finite time. That's enough for us to use it in the proof. To get a handle on what this matrix looks like, Table 2.5 shows the fundamental matrices for $|X| = 3$, $|Y| = 2$ and $|X| = 2$, $|Y| = 3$.

Table 2.5(a) $|X| = 3$, $|Y| = 2$

	f_0	f_1	f_2	f_3	f_4	f_5	f_6	f_7
x_0	y_0	y_0	y_0	y_0	y_1	y_1	y_1	y_1
x_1	y_0	y_0	y_1	y_1	y_0	y_0	y_1	y_1
x_2	y_0	y_1	y_0	y_1	y_0	y_1	y_0	y_1

Table 2.5(b) $|X| = 2$, $|Y| = 3$

	f_0	f_1	f_2	f_3	f_4	f_5	f_6	f_7	f_8
x_0	y_0	y_0	y_0	y_1	y_1	y_1	y_2	y_2	y_2
x_1	y_0	y_1	y_2	y_0	y_1	y_2	y_0	y_1	y_2

An important thing to note about the fundamental matrix is that each column of the fundamental matrix is distinct. Similarly, each row of the fundamental matrix is distinct.

SAQ 2.10

Why can't we have two identical columns, or two identical rows, in the fundamental matrix?

ANSWER..

Each column represents a definition of an element of F. If two columns are the same, it means that there are two elements of F that are the same. But we defined F as the set of distinct mappings from X to Y, so every element of F is distinct. This means that every column of the fundamental matrix is distinct. A similar argument applies for the rows.

The fundamental matrix encapsulates the fundamental features of any optimisation problem. We can think of it as a very simple game played between you and me. I choose a particular column in the matrix (representing the problem we're tackling). Without knowing what I've chosen, you have to choose a row (a strategy for addressing the problem). The element in the matrix at the junction of this row and column gives the pay-off, or how well our chosen strategy performs on that column. Obviously, you want to select the strategy that performs the best, that maximises our pay-off. Given that you don't know which column I've chosen, you're reduced to choosing the row that has the highest expected pay-off. You need to find a row of the fundamental matrix that has a higher-than-average number of high-value pay-offs, thereby increasing the odds that I'll have chosen a column that pays out well for you. Unfortunately, it's easy to show that every pay-off value occurs exactly the same number of times in each row.

The proof is fairly simple. Given that the fundamental matrix contains $|Y|$ different elements distributed over $|Y|^{|X|}$ columns, each y appears, on average, $|Y|^{|X|}/|Y| = |Y|^{|X|-1}$ times. If some particular y appears more often than that in a row, then at least one other y must appear less often in the same row. So, let's pick a row i, corresponding to your high-performing optimisation algorithm, and some arbitrary y (to illustrate this, we'll take the matrix shown in Table 2.5(a) and the x_1 row). We can now form a sub-matrix of the fundamental matrix by choosing only those columns where $F_{ij} = y$ (let's choose y_1). As all the columns in the fundamental matrix are unique, all the columns in the sub-matrix are also unique (see Table 2.6(a)). As all the values in the ith row are the same (our chosen y), if we eliminate our chosen row from the sub-matrix, all the columns will remain unique. Our sub-matrix now represents all the mappings from $|X| - 1$ strategies to $|Y|$ pay-offs (see Table 2.6(b)). As I showed above, this sub-matrix contains, at most, $|Y|^{|X|-1}$ elements. As we can apply this strategy to every y, it follows that no y can appear more often than $|Y|^{|X|-1}$ times in F, so every y appears exactly $|Y|^{|X|-1}$ times.

Table 2.6(a)

	f_2	f_3	f_6	f_7
x_0	y_0	y_0	y_1	y_1
x_1	y_1	y_1	y_1	y_1
x_2	y_0	y_1	y_0	y_1

Table 2.6(b)

	f_2	f_3	f_6	f_7
x_0	y_0	y_0	y_1	y_1
x_2	y_0	y_1	y_0	y_1

Given that each pay-off appears exactly the same number of times in each row, it follows that the average pay-off in each row is the same.

Exercise 2.5

Prove that the average pay-off for each row in the fundamental matrix is the same. Find an expression for that pay-off.

Answer..

Since each y appears $|Y|^{|X|-1}$ times in each row, the row sum for each row is:

$$\sum_{j=0}^{F-1} F_{ij} = \sum_{k=0}^{Y-1} y_k |Y|^{|X|-1}$$

and the row average is:

$$\frac{1}{|F|} \sum_{j=0}^{F-1} F_{ij} = \frac{1}{|Y|^{|X|}} \sum_{k=0}^{Y-1} y_k |Y|^{|X|-1} = \frac{1}{|Y|} \sum_{k=0}^{Y-1} y_k$$

This is, essentially, the No Free Lunch (NFL) theorem. Every row of the fundamental matrix has the same average pay-off. This means that every optimisation strategy performs exactly as well as any other, when averaged over all problems. This doesn't seem to be a big deal until you remember that random search counts as a strategy. NFL tells us that nothing we do can ever be better than pure, blind luck.

That's a happy thought, isn't it?

6.2 | Sidestepping the No Free Lunch theorem, or running away before the maitre d' catches us

At first, the NFL theorem seems surprising: optimisation strategies like GAs do seem to perform much better than approaches like using burnt sheep scapulae. What's going on?

The key thing about NFL is that it applies when we average it over the space of all possible problems. If we're not interested in solving all possible problems, perhaps we can choose a strategy that works better on our chosen subset, at the expense of performing poorly on the problems we're not interested in.

It seems that we're probably doing this with the optimisation problems we generally tackle. This is perhaps most obvious when we look at GAs, but the same argument can be applied to artificial neural networks (ANNs) and other optimisation strategies. During the optimisation process, our chosen strategy generally goes through a series of iterations (generations, eons), seeing how it performs. This performance evaluation is generally done by calling a simple fitness function or similar. The key thing to realise is that the fitness function encapsulates all the important features of the problem. Essentially, the problem becomes defined by the fitness function.

If we look at the space of all possible fitness functions, we find that most of them will be vast. A fitness function maps inputs to outputs. The most straightforward way of doing this is for the fitness function to be a simple look-up table with one entry for each input. As we saw in the discussion of Markov processes above, the number of inputs to the fitness function will normally be a very large number, which makes writing the appropriate look-up table prohibitively expensive to create. Instead, we want to be able to write a small program that can calculate the fitness of a given input. To allow this to happen, we have to be able to compress all the information in the original look-up table into the program: both must contain the same information if they are to be equivalent. It turns out that most such functions contain so much information that the only programs that are equivalent to them are not much smaller than the look-up tables: there is little or no regularity in the fitness function that can be exploited by simple program logic.

In other words, we're generally not interested in the space of all possible problems. It seems that we're often interested in problems that contain much less information than is possible; problems that contain regularity and structure. If that is the case, then it may be possible to sidestep the NFL theorem by restricting our optimisation efforts to just this small sub-class of problems.

Of course, this insight doesn't tell us anything about the size of this set of problems, nor does it say anything about which optimisation strategies are best for which problems. But it does suggest that there won't be one single optimisation process that will be better than all others. It seems that we'll have to know a little bit about a lot of approaches for some time to come.

Summary of Unit 2

In the beginning of this unit, I presented a set of requirements for any theory of GAs. A good theory should allow us to:

▶ make the GA better (e.g. how much crossover to allow);

▶ choose the most appropriate representation of a problem (e.g. what's in a genome?);

▶ decide whether a GA is a good way of solving a particular problem.

Now I've looked at a number of theories, I can reflect on the efficacy of those theories in explaining how GAs work.

Schema theory was, for a long time, the accepted definition of how GAs work. The problem is that it isn't a very good theory. Direct tests of the predictive power of the theory (in the shape of the Royal Road tests) showed that GAs don't really behave like they are processing schemata. Further examination of the theory brought into doubt the strength of conclusions about exponentially increasing trials and the nature of schemata themselves for non-binary genomes. In any case, schema theory doesn't say much about how to configure a particular GA for best effect.

GAs are stochastic processes; Markov processes are also stochastic processes. It seemed like a match made in heaven. This approach even paid off in that it showed that including mutation in a GA ensures that it will never converge on an optimal solution. This prompted the idea of including elitism in a GA, to ensure that the best individuals really do survive. However, the transition matrices needed for the analyses of GAs as Markov processes turned out to be too vast to be useful. Again, little came out of this theory that can be directly applied to improving the performance of GAs in practice.

Finally, I looked at statistical mechanics. This seems promising as there are explicit mathematical relationships between the action of various operations and their effects on the population. The problem is that the approach depends critically on the precise effects of mutation and crossover on the fitness of an individual, and this can be very difficult to quantify.

There are other approaches to the development of a theory of GAs, but they all suffer from the same problems of little direct relevance to practical problems.

We finished this unit by looking at the No Free Lunch theorem, which shows that GAs are no better, and no worse, than any other problem-solving method, including random chance. However, the NFL theorem doesn't necessarily hold for particular subsets of problems, but we seemingly have no way of predicting what those subsets are.

The next unit considers how the idea of evolution can be applied more widely. In particular, it looks at genetic programming, where problem-solving programs are developed using evolutionary techniques, and evolutionary robotics, where the hard problem of robot control is solved by evolving, rather than directly coding, a neural-network based solution.

Before moving on, look back at the learning outcomes for this unit and check these against what you think you can now do. Return to any section of the unit if you feel you need to.

Unit 3: Artificial evolution

CONTENTS

Introduction to Unit 3

In Unit 1 of this block I reviewed the basic principles of GAs, and in Unit 2 covered a bit of the theory underlying them. The chief *use* you've seen so far – for GAs, and evolutionary computation generally – has been for the solution of optimisation problems. In this final unit of the block, I will be looking at two other areas in which the evolutionary principles of GAs have been applied: *genetic programming* and *evolutionary robotics*. Both of these are major areas of research endeavour, with many hundreds of active researchers contributing to them. All I can hope to do, therefore, is to give you an insight into the direction work in each of these fields has taken.

Section 2 is devoted, then, to the principles of genetic programming. There I will discuss how the GA principles you learned about in Unit 1 of this block have been applied to the evolution, not of solutions to optimisation problems, but to *computer programs* themselves. I will cover the questions of how a computer program can be represented on a genome and then subjected to the usual processes of crossover and mutation to breed new and improved varieties. The section concludes with a short case study illustrating a practical application of genetic programming.

Section 3 deals with *evolutionary robotics*. Here the aim is to apply the same evolutionary principles to develop controllers for reactive robots. Since most modern robotic control systems are based on some form of neural network, the problem boils down to evolving, rather than specifying and training, a neural network. I start by looking at what it means to evolve a neural system, and consider the options available. The rest of the section is then devoted to a series of case studies demonstrating how some of these options have been taken up in research systems. This will lead us into quite advanced theoretical questions in artificial evolution, such as co-evolution, the interaction between evolution and learning, and the mapping between genotype and phenotype.

I'll end the unit with a summary and some concluding remarks.

What you need to study this unit

You will need the following course components, and will need to use your computer and internet connection for some of the exercises.

▶   this Block 5 text
▶   the course DVD.

LEARNING OUTCOMES FOR UNIT 3

After studying this unit you will be able to:

3.1 draw diagrams illustrating how a computer program can be represented as either a tree, a linear structure or a graph;

3.2 write a paragraph, illustrated with diagrams, explaining how crossover and mutation can be applied to representations of a computer program;

3.3 briefly explain the distinction between the distal and the proximal view of robotic behaviour;

3.4 draw diagrams illustrating the principles of Braitenberg vehicles and neural robotic controllers;

3.5 write a set of bullet points tracing the manner in which the weights of a simple neural controller for a robot can be evolved;

3.6 write a paragraph justifying the need for modularity and internal states within robotic controllers;

3.7 write brief definitions of the *bootstrap problem*, the *Baldwin effect* and the *genotype to phenotype mapping problem*;

3.8 outline the use of incremental evolution in evolutionary robotics;

3.9 write an account of how competitive co-evolution can be used to address the bootstrap problem;

3.10 write brief definitions of the *cycling problem* and the *Red Queen Problem* as they arise in competitive co-evolution;

3.11 write a short reflective essay discussing the interaction of adaptation and selection in evolutionary robotics;

3.12 write a description of one indirect approach to the mapping of genotype onto phenotype in evolutionary robotics.

2 Genetic programming

As you've learned, the most common use of GAs is in optimisation problems, where the genomes represent possible solutions to the problem. **Genetic programming** (**GP**) is a related field of research, where genomes are set up to express and evolve *computer programs*. Computer programming is a difficult, arduous and error-prone activity. It is also immensely expensive. It can only be performed well by highly trained and skilled individuals, who command high rates of pay. In Block 1, I made the point that the human impulse has always been to develop tools to assist us with difficult tasks. And so we have done with programming: today we have a panoply of integrated development environments (IDEs), compilers, debuggers and human–computer interface (HCI) development systems at our command. What could be a more natural goal for AI, then, than to take this one stage further and develop computer systems that are themselves able to write correct and efficient programs – automatically? One branch of the search for such systems is GP.

2.1 Origins

For further information, see Friedberg (1958).

The origins of GP go back further than those of GAs. As long ago as 1958, Richard Friedberg designed a system to write novel computer programs to solve simple problems. Programs in Friedberg's system contained sixty-four individual instructions, each of which could perform an operation on sixty-four bits of data or jump to another instruction. The system was divided into Herman, the hypothetical learner, and the Teacher.

At the beginning of each simulation, the Teacher would place data into the memory and then give Herman a set of random instructions. Herman would start to execute these in order, until it reached the sixty-fourth instruction. If the final output stored in memory matched that expected by the Teacher then Herman was said to have succeeded. If Herman's final result differed, or if it failed to execute sixty-four instructions within a time limit (maybe by entering an infinite loop), then Herman had 'failed' that test.

Herman's instructions could be altered in the following ways:

▶ through *routine change*, where an individual instruction could be replaced by an alternative;

▶ by *random change*, in which random individual instructions were replaced by new random instructions.

Routine changes resulted from the relative success of two instructions at specific points being compared, the more successful instruction being favoured in subsequent runs. Random changes permitted Herman to explore a diverse range of possible solutions. The rate at which changes occurred was governed by the success of individual instructions: those that contributed to a successful solution had their successfulness incremented at the end of a simulation; those that were part of an unsuccessful solution were subject to 'criticism' and could be changed.

Figure 3.1 shows Herman's progress at producing a solution over twenty blocks each of 10 000 trials, i.e. a total of 200 000 trials. You can see that there is a rapid increase in the rate of success (it managed just twenty-six successes out of 10 000 attempts in the first block), but progress largely stalled between blocks 6 and 15. Friedberg commented that the early increase was explained by Herman eliminating

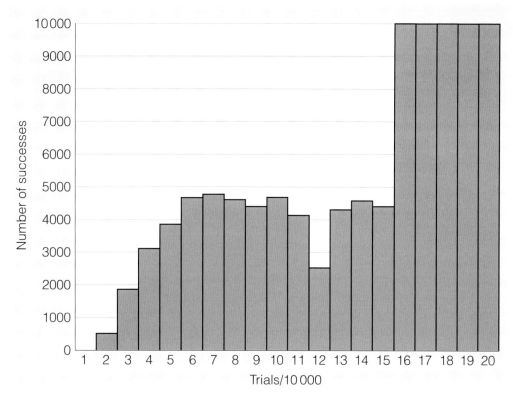

Figure 3.1   Herman's progress in developing a successful program. Each division along the horizontal axis represents 10 000 runs

programs that never ran to completion within their time limit. By the end of block 5, 90% of Herman's programs were completing, but only about half of them were successful. At some point in block 15 Herman stumbled across a near perfect solution, which it then exploited for the remainder of the experiment.

Friedberg explored many aspects of his system over millions of trials. Herman (and its sibling, Sherman) was consistently able to 'learn' successful programs. However, as Friedberg admitted, the scope of the programs was extremely limited. Most significantly, though, Friedberg had framed the central problem of machine learning in a manner completely recognisable to modern practitioners:

> If we are ever to make a machine that will speak, understand or translate human languages, solve mathematical problems ... practice a profession or direct an organization, either we must reduce these activities to a science so exact that we can tell a machine precisely how to go about doing them or we must develop a machine that can do things without being told precisely how ...
>
> ... The machine might be designed to gravitate toward those procedures which most often elicit from us a favorable response. We could teach this machine to perform a task even though we could not describe a precise method for performing it, provided only that we understood the task well enough to be able to ascertain whether or not it had been done successfully.

Source: Friedberg (1958)

Friedberg's work should have given impetus to many similar projects, but the 1960s saw his work sidelined by the rise of knowledge-based systems. It was only much later, towards the end of the 1980s, that experimenters began to re-explore the idea of automated generation of computer programs, and to investigate the potential of GP.

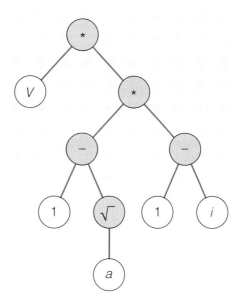

Figure 3.3   Tree representation of the expression in Exercise 3.1

It takes a slight effort of the imagination, but you can see that any well-formed computer program could, in principle, be represented as a tree in this way.

Linear structures

The simplest representation for a genetic program is as a linear structure, the program beginning execution at one end and terminating at the other. This structure closely resembles the representation of a program in a physical computer: a series of instructions manipulating a set of memory locations that mimic the registers of a CPU. The only exception to the pattern of linear execution is a jump instruction that allows the program to skip a number of instructions backward or forward. Unlike trees, in linear structures the contents of any register can be read or written to by any instruction – memory is global. An example of a linear structure is shown in Figure 3.4.

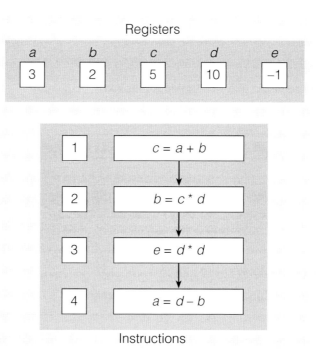

Figure 3.4   A linear representation of a GA. The program is executed (in this case) in sequence from top to bottom and operates on a series of registers (labelled from a to e)

Linear structures make for extremely fast genetic programs. It is possible to represent individual instructions in the underlying hardware's machine code and to store values directly in CPU registers. Speed is gained at the expense of flexibility, though – a program designed for a particular hardware configuration is unlikely to work on a different machine.

Graphs

The most recent innovation in GP representation is *graphs*. You've met graphs in Block 3, but just to recap, try this question.

SAQ 3.2

What is a graph, as I used the term in Block 3?

ANSWER..

A graph, $G = (N,A)$, is a set of *nodes* $N = \{n_1, n_2 \dots n_i\}$ connected by a set of weighted *edges* $A = N = \{a_1, a_2 \dots a_i\}$.

In a graphical representation of a program, the edges represent paths of execution. In contrast to the largely sequential nature of linear representations, graphs allow programs to jump between instructions, and so permit a richer programming style – incorporating recursion, for example – than linear structures or trees.

Figure 3.5 illustrates a graph-theoretic representation of a program that could be embodied in a GP. The *Start* and *End* nodes mark, respectively, the beginning and end of the program. A program stack is used to transfer values between operations and serves as local memory: for instance, the result of a + operation is pushed on to the top of the stack, a subsequent / operation will pop two values from the top of the stack.

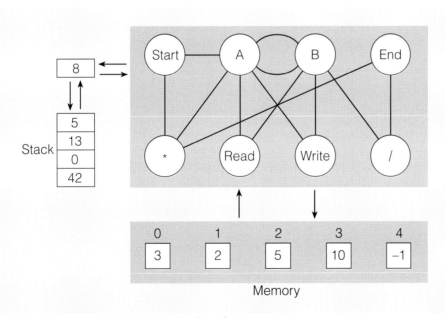

Figure 3.5   A graph-theoretic representation of a program.

The stack is supplemented by a block of external memory. Information is read from memory using a dedicated *Read* operation and written back to memory in a corresponding *Write* operation. The memory can be accessed from any node in the program graph.

Nodes perform two major tasks:

▶ They perform some operation on either the stack (pushing values onto the stack or popping them from it) or on main memory (reading from or writing to it).

▶ They select the next node to be executed using decision logic based on the value of the topmost item in the stack or on the contents of a location in memory.

So these are the three main schemes of representation for a computer program. Now let's move on to discuss how computer programs may be evolved.

2.4 | A genetic program

John R. Koza, one of the earliest exponents and most persistent champions of GP recommends that, to build a genetic program, the following decisions should be made, in order:

▶ the set of terminals;

▶ the set of functions;

▶ the fitness measure;

▶ the evolutionary parameters.

From now on let's consider these in the context of a GP for a classic AI problem, one you've met several times before: planning in a Blocks World. This version of the problem has nine blocks, each inscribed with a letter. From any random initial state, the task is to stack the blocks in such an order that a word is correctly spelled out (see Figure 3.6) – only one real word is possible.

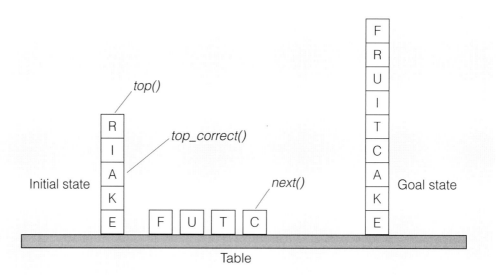

Figure 3.6   The Blocks World

The terminals

Three sensor functions monitor the state of the Blocks World and return values to the program. They are:

▶ *top()* – returns the letter of the top block of the stack;

▶ *top_correct()* – returns the letter of a block in the stack such that it and all the letters below it are in the right order;

▶ *next()* – returns the value of the next block that should be above *top_correct()*.

So, in the state illustrated in Figure 3.6, *top*() returns 'R', *top-correct*() returns 'A' and *next*() returns 'C'. The terminals are thus these three functions:

$T = \{top(x), top\_correct(x), next()\}$

Note there are no variables or constants in the set.

The functions

The program draws on a set of only five functions:

$F = \{move\_stack(x), move\_table(x), do\_until(work,term), not(x), equal(x,y)\}$

where:

▶ *move_stack*(x) has the side effect of moving block x to the top of the stack. Returns TRUE if this is possible, FALSE otherwise.

▶ *move_table*(x) has the side effect of moving the top block of the stack to the table, if x is anywhere in the stack. Returns TRUE if this is possible, FALSE otherwise.

▶ *do_until*(a,b) repeats a until b evaluates to TRUE then returns TRUE. Artificially time limited to twenty-five iterations, it returns FALSE if timed out.

▶ *not*(x) and *equal*(x,y) are the Boolean functions NOT and EQUAL.

These functions are all closed. Armed with them, it is now possible to start evolving a program.

The evolution of genetic programs then proceeds in much the same manner as with GAs, which I discussed in Unit 1. Remind yourselves of this.

SAQ 3.3

Sum up in your own words the main stages through which a GA passes. Look back if you need to.

ANSWER...

Here is a brief summary of the steps:

1   Create a population of randomly generated genomes, each representing a possible solution to the problem.

2   Create a mating pool of the same size as the population by:

    2.i   applying the fitness function to every genome;

    2.ii   randomly selecting pairs of genomes from the population, based on the biased roulette wheel;

    2.iii mutating genes in the mating pool (alternatively, mutation may occur at the step 3.iii, or not at all).

3   Build a new population (Generation n + 1) by:

    3.i   selecting pairs of genomes for crossover (those not selected pass directly into the new population);

    3.ii   mutating genes on crossover (alternatively, mutation may occur at step 2.iii, or not at all).

4   Go back to step 2.

The process terminates at the point where very fit individuals dominate the population.

Note that the initial population in the case of GP consists of a set of computer programs, rather than bit or character strings.

The fitness measure

In this example, the fitness of a program clearly depends on its ability to create a correct stack from some initial state. However, since there are millions of possible initial states, it is hardly feasible to test them all. Consequently, fitness was measured on the ability of a program to produce the goal from 166 statistically sampled initial states. Obviously then, the highest possible fitness score would be 166 (able to generate the right stack from all of them) and the lowest 0 (no correct stacks produced).

The evolutionary parameters

The initial population size and other decisions depend largely on the problem in hand. In our example, evolution began with a randomly generated population of 500 programs.

Let's now consider further the question of genomes, crossover and mutation in the context of GPs. I'll concentrate almost exclusively on tree-structured programs, since these are what our example uses.

Genomes

GPs are not generally encoded as bit strings, as in GAs. Instead, the crossover and mutation operators work directly on the program tree. It is possible to build the trees of the initial population in a number of ways, divisible into two broad, contrasting categories:

▶ *Grow* methods build a tree from the root by randomly selecting functions and terminals until every branch ends with a terminal. Trees developed using this method tend to be irregular and may be too impoverished to evolve useful programs from.

▶ *Full* methods populate a tree only with functions until it reaches a maximum permitted depth, whereupon it is finished with terminal nodes. Every branch reaches the maximum depth so the tree is regular.

It is possible to combine these two methods in order to encourage greater diversity in the original population; one method is called 'ramped-half-and-half'. A selection of populations of trees are grown, each population having a different maximum depth. In each population half of the trees are built by grow methods, half by full methods.

In our example, trees were generated using *grow* methods. As one would expect, most were useless, so ill-formed that they performed no actions at all. One or two were well-formed enough to work and even to score more than 0 fitness. Figure 3.7 shows an example.

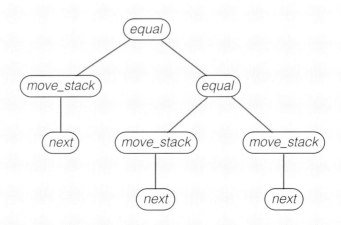

Figure 3.7   Randomly generated program

Exercise 3.2

What effect would this program have if it were run? What would its fitness be?
Remember to evaluate the tree depth-first.

Discussion ....

The program will move up to three 'next' blocks from the table onto the stack. It will
therefore produce the goal state from these possible initial states: 'I T C A K E', 'U I T C A
K E', 'R U I T C A K E' or 'F R U I T C A K E', i.e. six, seven, eight or nine blocks
already stacked in the right order. There are thus four initial states in which this will give
the goal state, so its fitness is 4.

Crossover

Just as in GAs, trees are selected to go into a mating pool, and then pairs of trees
are picked randomly from the pool and tested for crossover (revisit Unit 1 to refresh
your memory, if necessary). If the test process determines that crossover should
take place, then random sub-trees of the parents are swapped between the two
genomes and the new children pass into the population of the next generation.
I've illustrated this in Figure 3.8.

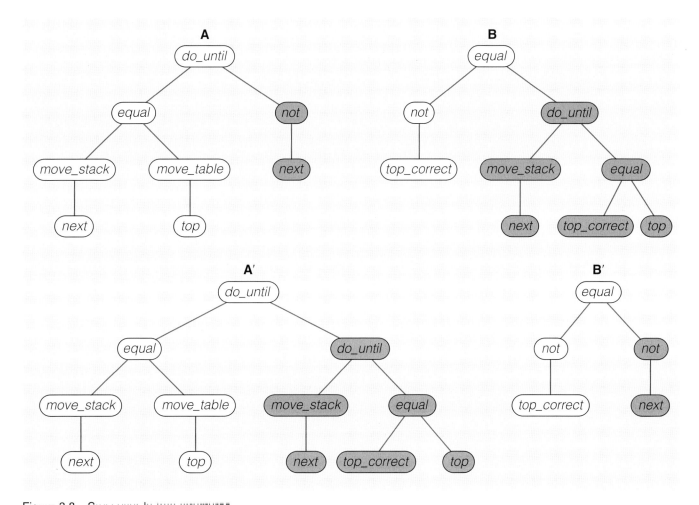

Figure 3.8   Crossover in tree structures

Mutation

Mutation generally operates on single genomes and can take place during or after crossover. The results of tree mutations tend to be more extensive than mutation in bit string genomes. When a tree has been selected for mutation, a random node in it is selected and the sub-tree below that point is replaced. Compare this with a conventional GA where mutation flips a single bit.

The replacement sub-tree is generated randomly using the same procedures that created the original population. This might simply replace one terminal node with a new terminal or build an entirely new tree – therefore mutation can be responsible for gross changes in the structure of an individual genome.

Figure 3.9 shows two evolved 'programs' that are both capable of scoring maximum fitness. However, (b) is extremely inefficient, simply unstacking every block to the table and then stacking them up again in the correct order. (a) is an efficient solution. It would of course be possible to modify the fitness function to score for efficiency along with correctness.

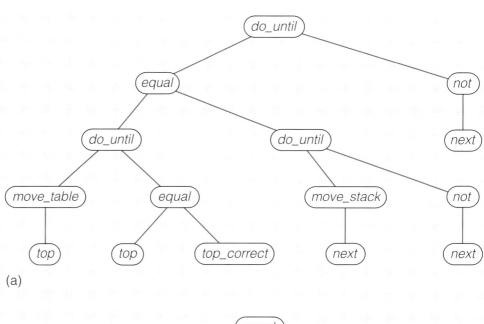

(a)

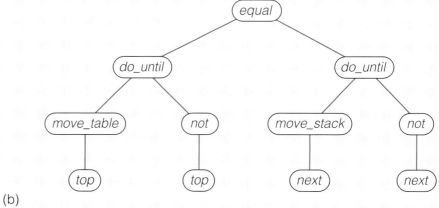

(b)

Figure 3.9   Two evolved programs

2.5 Applications of GP

GP has been successfully applied in numerous areas. One of these is the evolution of programs capable of playing games. Since computer game-playing has figured so prominently in the history of AI, let's look at one example of such a system.

Case Study 3.1: Playing backgammon

In a recent experiment, Yaniv Azaria and Moshe Sipper (2005) evolved a computer program for playing backgammon at a high level. Hugely popular throughout the Middle East, like chess, backgammon is a board game of great skill. Unlike chess, though, it is partly a game of chance, where the outcome may hang on the throw of dice. It is a game of great antiquity: a board resembling a backgammon board, dated to about 3000 BCE, was recently found in the ruins of a bronze-age settlement in present-day Iran. Vast sums are won and lost every year gambling on backgammon.

Backgammon is a simpler game than chess, but it is not necessary to understand its rules in any detail to appreciate Azaria and Sipper's work. It is a game for two players, white and black, with a board and starting position illustrated in Figure 3.10. The aim is for each player to move their counters around the board, from point to point, in the direction shown. Once all a player's counters are in their home board (see Figure 3.10), that player can then start to 'bear off': that is, start to remove their counters from the board. The distance counters can be moved, and whether or not they can be borne off, depends on the throw of two dice. The player who removes all his counters first is the winner.

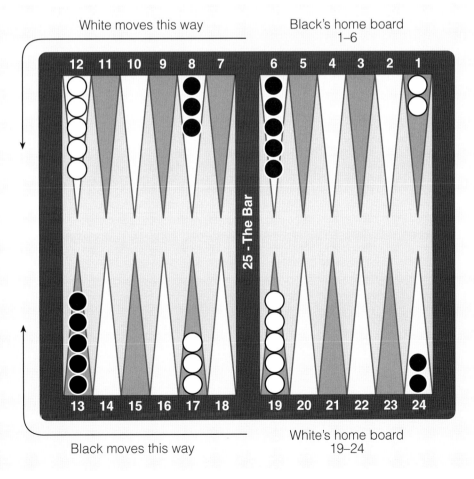

Figure 3.10   The backgammon board

As you can see, the players' counters have to move past one another to reach their respective goals. During this phase of the game – the *contact phase* – there is much scope for players to block one another's progress (as it is not possible to land on a point with two or more opposing counters on it); and for 'hitting' – landing on a point with only one enemy counter on it, known as a 'blot', means the enemy counter is removed from the board and placed on the Bar, to wait there to start its journey again from the beginning. Once the counters of each colour have passed one another, and since they cannot move backwards, a new phase begins – the *race phase*, in which players are in a straight race to be the first to bear all their counters off.

Azaria and Sipper's idea was *not* to build a system to do a conventional search of the game tree, which is as massive as that of chess. Rather, they aimed to evolve a program, *GP-Gammon*, that would take the current state of the board and value of the dice thrown, evaluate the board position that would arise immediately after making each possible move, given the value thrown, and award each position a numerical score. The move leading to the position with the highest score would then be selected.

Since the program was required to return one single value for each possible board position, it could be treated as a single function, best represented as a tree. In fact Azaria and Sipper used two trees, one for the contact phase and one for the race phase. Following Koza's principles for GP practice, described above, let's now briefly review the decisions they made in each case.

The set of terminals

Recall that the terminals in a GP are the specific values it will work with. In the case of *GP-Gammon*, these were either floating-point numbers or whole numbers between 1 and 25 inclusive (as there are twenty-five points on the board, including the Bar), randomly generated. But remember that terminals can also be functions, returning important values. In the case of *GP-Gammon*, the researchers chose a number of:

▶ query functions, which returned specific information about board positions;

▶ board evaluation functions, returning general information about the board as a whole.

Examples of some of these functions are given in Table 3.1.

Table 3.1 Examples of functions used in *GP-Gammon*

Function	Description
Player_exposed(n)	Returns 1 if player has exactly one counter at location *n*, otherwise returns 0
Player_blocked(n)	Returns 1 if player has two or more counters at location *n*, otherwise returns 0
Enemy_blocked(n)	Returns 1 if enemy has two or more counters at location *n*, otherwise returns 0
Player_position(n)	Returns the number of counters at position *n*
Enemy_pip	Returns the number of moves the enemy has to make to win
Total_hit_prob	Returns the sum of the probability of being hit over all blots

There were eleven such terminal functions in all. Different functions were chosen from this set for each tree.

The set of functions

In addition to these, the researchers chose a number of general-purpose functions, which could be used in both trees. Examples are given in Table 3.2.

Table 3.2 General-purpose functions used in *GP-Gammon*

Function	Description
If(*b*,*f1*,*f2*)	If *b* is true, returns *f1*, otherwise returns *f2*
Greater(*f1*,*f2*)	Returns 1 if *f1* is greater than *f2*, otherwise returns 0

A total of nine general-purpose functions were used.

The fitness measure

Games of backgammon are generally short, and the outcome depends to some extent on chance, so the result of a single game would be a poor measure of fitness. Therefore, each solution was assessed by being required to play a hundred-game tournament against *Pubeval*, a publicly available backgammon-playing program that is much used as a benchmark against which to match other programs.

As fitness was assessed by machine playing machine, evaluation time could be kept relatively short.

The evolutionary parameters

Azaria and Sipper settled on a population size of 128 genomes, each representing a possible program tree. The initial random population of program trees was built using the ramped-half-and-half technique described above, by picking a random integer between *min-depth* and *max-depth* and growing a tree to this depth. Evolution automatically ended after 500 generations.

To govern the evolutionary process itself, individuals were selected and mated in the conventional way using four operators:

▶ identity – one individual passes to the next generation with no change;

▶ tree crossover (see above);

▶ sub-tree mutation (see above);

▶ number mutation – alter every number within a sub-tree below a node selected at random.

One of these operators was repeatedly chosen at random and applied to one or two genomes, until the new population reached 128. Genomes were selected for the mating pool using a method called **tournament selection**, in which a small subset of the population was repeatedly chosen at random and the fittest individual in this set chosen each time.

Results 1

Every four generations, the best program in the population played a 1000-game tournament against *Pubeval* and the results were logged. After 500 generations, the best program achieved about a 40% score, which is considered good, but not outstanding (*Pubeval* is a very strong program).

This was in Unit 4 of
Block 3.

Co-evolution

The researchers then hit on a much better idea – one which you've met before in Hillis' work on breeding sorting networks, and one which you will meet again shortly. Instead of evaluating the fitness of programs against one 'champion' external opponent, the evolutionary process was driven by *self-learning* – getting programs to play *against each other*.

It worked like this:

1   Select a tournament of n individuals, where n is an even number.
2   Divide the tournament into pairs and make each pair play a fifty-game tournament against one another.
3   Set the fitness of all losers to $1/n$.
4   Divide the $n/2$ winners into pairs and conduct another tournament.
5   Set the fitness of the losers to $1/(n/2)$.
6   Continue this process until a champion emerges.

The immediate assignment of low fitness to half the population at step 3 was found to prevent premature convergence.

Results 2

Once again, the best program in the population of every fourth generation played a 1000-game tournament against *Pubeval*. After 500 generations, the best program achieved about a 57% score, among the best results ever recorded.

Exercise 3.3

Why do you think the self-learning method of driving the evolution produced so much better results?

Discussion ....

Probably the answer is the reasonably obvious one. Despite its apparent simplicity, backgammon is a game of deep strategy. It seems likely that, since the programs evolved through a fitness assessment based only on performance against *Pubeval*, they became overfitted to that program's strategy. In reality, good players of any game become good by playing against a variety of opponents.

The self-learning strategy adopted by Azaria and Sipper is known as *co-evolution*. You will meet it again in the next section.

Computer Exercise 3.1

In this activity, you'll look at a demonstration GA tool and use it to explore how GP works in practice. Load up and complete Computer Exercise 3.1 on the course DVD.

3 Robots, neural networks and evolution

3.1 Background

In this final section of Block 5, three major threads in M366 come together: robotics, evolutionary computation and neural networks. From Block 3 onwards, our theme has been *natural intelligence*. In Block 3 itself, you learned that one of the most realistic and potentially fruitful paths for investigating natural intelligence and for building AI systems is *robotics*. But naturally intelligent beings – ants, lobsters, chimpanzees and humanity itself – are, we believe, products of evolutionary forces. So could evolutionary computation be applied to robotics? Instead of *engineering* robotic controllers, as the Stanford researchers (Shakey) and the MIT Lab (Toto) had done, might it be possible to *evolve* them? And if it is possible, what would the results tell us about natural intelligence and about evolution itself? And what would be their significance for AI?

Let's start with a quick recap of some basic ideas about recent trends in robotics, which I presented earlier in the course.

SAQ 3.4

Try to recall some of the main features of behaviour-based robotics that you met in Block 3, Unit 4. There's no need to go into much detail: just jot down some of the basic ideas.

ANSWER...

I thought the main ideas were these:

▶ Internally, a robot is constructed out of a set of basic *behaviours*.

▶ These behaviours collaborate in parallel to link information from the robot's sensors directly to its actuators: the SENSE–PLAN–ACT cycle is replaced with a SENSE–ACT cycle.

▶ Behaviours are often arranged in layers, with one layer *subsuming* the other. Subsumption of a lower layer by a higher one means that the higher layer will only intervene if the lower layer cannot solve a problem unassisted.

Because of the direct linkage between perception and action, with no intervening planning, these kinds of architecture are sometimes called *reactive* models.

The reactive approach to robotic design, based on biological theories of insect locomotion and control has been very successful, but there are problems with it.

Behaviour

One useful way of thinking about robot behaviour is to distinguish between two possible perspectives on it – the **distal view** and the **proximal view**:

▶ Imagine you are watching a rubbish-collecting robot going about its business. It moves through its environment, avoiding walls and obstacles, moving towards discarded beer bottles and litter, picking them up, etc. – in other words, it performs a number of complex behaviours. This is the *distal* view of the robot's behaviour.

This distinction was suggested by the AI scientists Noel Sharkey and Jan Heemskerk.

▶ Now imagine the same set of tasks from the point of view of the robot engineer, or the robot itself. Performing a complex action like picking up a bottle involves an intricate set of interactions among low-level internal behaviours and the environment. A description of these interactions makes up the *proximal* view of the overall distal behaviour.

This distinction is just another version of one that comes up time and again in the sciences of human and animal behaviour. Fields such as psychology, anthropology and ethology offer *distal* descriptions of behaviour, and have developed specialised vocabularies for this purpose. Other fields, such as neuroscience and genetics, try to account for these same behaviours in low-level terms – the interactions of nerve cells and genes. They take a *proximal* perspective, and use their own dedicated terminologies. Reconciling the two distinct levels of description, these completely different vocabularies, is a problem science has come nowhere near cracking.

But the problem for roboticists is this. It is *very* difficult to design controllers that will generate complex distal behaviours. Because the robot's distal behaviour will result from an intricate set of internal interactions and interactions with the environment, and because a real-world environment is highly complex and dynamic itself, the correct decomposition of the system into modules and layers will certainly not be obvious, even for simple behaviour. Think back to the descriptions of the subsumption architecture I gave in Unit 4 of Block 3. In its final form, the internal architecture of a simple robot described there comprised fourteen behaviour modules, with a complicated pattern of signalling between them. Each module had to be very carefully designed, with a great deal of trial and error involved. The signals between them were finely tuned. The whole system needed to be intensively tested and tweaked before it worked satisfactorily. And the distal behaviour of the robot was, in the end, fairly uncomplicated: just wall-following and obstacle avoidance! If such an intensive engineering effort had to go into producing even relatively straightforward distal behaviour, imagine the problems in designing a more sophisticated robot, one capable of doing your housework, say.

Neural networks as robotic controllers

Maybe surprisingly, it is much easier to develop effective robotic controllers (for reasonably straightforward behaviour) that *don't* have elaborate internal modular architectures, using neural network techniques. In fact, a very sparse, homogeneous internal design can produce quite sophisticated distal behaviour. The best known cases of this are the famous **Braitenberg vehicles**.

They are named after Valentino Braitenberg, whose brilliant book *Vehicles: Experiments in synthetic psychology* laid down some of the founding principles of modern robotics.

Braitenberg vehicles are very simple robots without internal modular components. Instead, sensors are connected directly to actuators by connections of variable strength. Figure 3.11 shows a basic Braitenberg vehicle. (Braitenberg called this a Type 2 system.) Two light sensors, mounted at the front of the robot, are wired to the motors in the pattern shown. In this case, each connection is of positive strength: that is, the brighter the light falling on the sensor, the faster the connection will encourage the motor to run. Now consider this question.

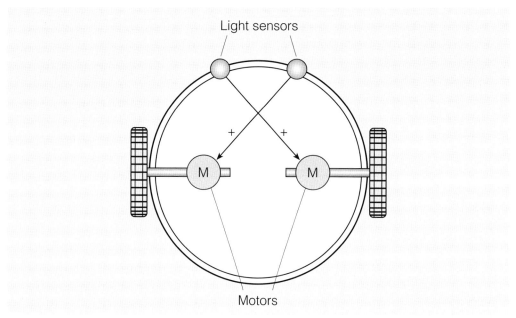

Figure 3.11 A Type 2 Braitenberg vehicle. The vehicle is represented as a circle, with one stylised wheel mounted on an axle at each side

Exercise 3.4

Suppose the robot depicted in Figure 3.11 is situated on a flat plane and – in the absence of any external stimulus – is programmed to move directly forward at a steady pace. Now suppose also that a light source is moving randomly around the plane. What will be the behaviour of the robot as it moves to within sensing distance of the light?

Discussion ....

The robot will *follow* the light wherever it leads. It works like this: if the source is positioned to one side of the robot, then a greater quantity of light will fall onto the sensor positioned on that side. This will cause the motor on the opposite side to the sensor to work harder than the other motor, causing the robot to turn towards the light.

So a controller of the utmost simplicity can lead to light-following behaviour. Braitenberg identified a number of classes of robotic vehicles of this general kind. In fact, this kind of internal organisation is one that you have met before in M366.

SAQ 3.5

Where in M366 have you seen something like this before?

ANSWER..

Beer's hexapodal walking robots are a more complex version of this sort of organisation. Recall that in these there were a number of different controllers and actuators, linked together by positive (excitatory) and negative (inhibitory) connections. Complex walking behaviour emerged from the interaction between these components.

You can see that the whole set-up is intensely reminiscent of a neural network, with its simple units connected by weighted links. Modular architectures may be difficult to design for robotic controllers, but homogeneous, uniform systems based on neural network principles can be set up much more easily. Their weights can then be set by hand or trained. Designers can simply let the principles of interaction, emergence and adaptation do the work for them.

Now, to return to my earlier question: can the techniques of evolutionary computation that I've been discussing in this block be of any use? Can we use GA techniques to *evolve* rather than *engineer* robotic control systems?

3.2 Evolving simple reactive robots

First, a practical issue. In evolving a robotic controller, does one work directly with physical robots or with computer simulations? There are advantages and drawbacks to either choice. A possible compromise is to evolve a simulated controller and then transfer it to a real robot. But there are, as you can probably guess, problems with such an approach:

▶ The physical sensors may return quite different results for the same environmental stimulus to those of their simulated counterparts.

▶ As Rodney Brookes pointed out, real sensors and actuators have very limited accuracy and are far from uniform: two supposedly identical sensors may give different readings for exactly the same stimulus.

For these reasons, researchers who favour simulation often deliberately build inaccuracies and noise into their systems.

Our aim is to evolve a simple robotic controller. The little controller I described in my discussion of Braitenberg vehicles above bears an obvious resemblance to a neural network, and in fact most controllers of modern reactive robots are today based on neural network principles. In effect, then, we are trying to evolve a neural network. So exactly what is it that gets evolved? There are three main possibilities:

▶ The most common and straightforward approach is to start with a fixed topology and evolve the system's *weights*. As you'll see shortly, in some cases this approach may yield better solutions than basic, adaptive training techniques such as backpropagation.

▶ Alternatively, we can try to evolve the *topology* itself, maybe evolving the weights later, or just relying on training. A very subtle variation on this strategy is to evolve a set of rules according to which a topology will grow under environmental influence.

▶ Finally, an approach you might not have thought of is to fix the topology and evolve a suitable *learning rule*.

You will meet examples of all these approaches in the discussions that follow. Let's start with a basic case study in which the first of these options was chosen.

Case Study 3.2: Simple evolution

Dario Floreano and Francesco Mondada (1994) report an experiment with the evolution of a neural controller for a simple two-wheeled robot. The robot's task was an undemanding one: to negotiate the maze depicted in Figure 3.12.

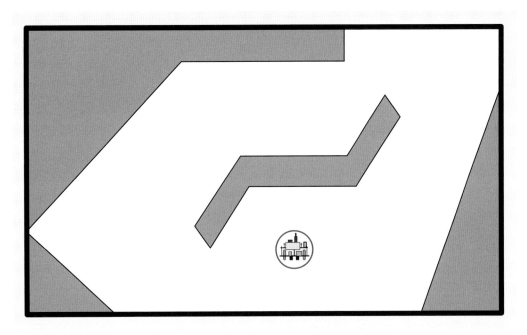

Figure 3.12   Maze used in Floreano and Mondada's 1994 experiment

The robot was a variation on the Braitenberg pattern, with eight infrared proximity sensors connected directly to the two motor controllers. I've illustrated this basic arrangement in Figure 3.13.

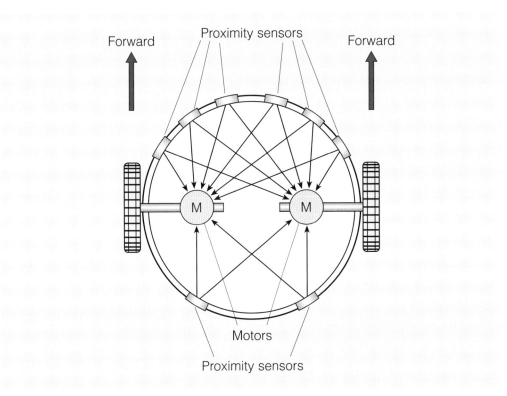

Figure 3.13   Internal wiring of Braitenberg robot

Connections were of variable strength and could be excitatory or inhibitory. This set-up was equivalent to the single-layer neural network that I've illustrated in Figure 3.14. But, as you can see, Floreano and Mondada elaborated on the basic Braitenberg structure of Figure 3.12 by adding recurrent connections and biases: the biases assured forward movement at all times, even in the absence of information from the sensors; the significance of the recurrent connections should become clear shortly. The activation functions of the two output units were sigmoids, adjusted to squash their output between –0.5 (backward rotation of the motor at full speed) and +0.5 (forward rotation of the motor at full speed). Operating in discrete time, the network read the sensors and applied impulse to the motors every 300 milliseconds (ms).

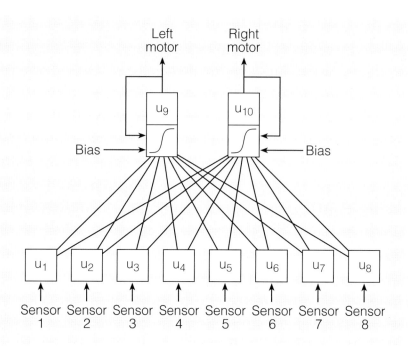

Figure 3.14   Neural controller in Floreano and Mondada's experiment

This was the basic set-up. As you can see from Figure 3.14, there are just twenty weights to find the right values for. Normally, one would expect to train a neural network of this kind with a standard technique such as vanilla backpropagation or epoch backpropagation though time (EBPTT). But instead – reasoning that this might yield better results – Floreano and Mondada took an evolutionary line and used the GA techniques you learned about in Unit 1 of this block to evolve the weights.

Here are some of the details:

1   *Genome*. With such a small weight set, no elaborate encoding of the potential solution was necessary. Each candidate was encoded in a simple string of twenty floating-point numbers, each representing a possible value for one of the weights.

2   *Fitness function*. Probably the most difficult aspect of any evolutionary robotic problem is deciding on a suitable fitness function. After some experiment, the researchers arrived at the following: fitness Φ was given by:

$$\Phi = V\left(1 - \sqrt{\Delta v}\right)(1 - i)$$

$$0 \le V \le 1$$
$$0 \le \Delta v \le 1 \qquad\qquad (3.1)$$
$$0 \le i \le 1$$

We can unpick this function as follows. The equation has three main terms:

▶ V is the total of the average speeds of rotation of the two wheels. The average rotation speed of the left and right wheels are added together (using absolute values, so if the left wheel rotates backwards at an average speed of –0.3 and the right wheel forward at an average speed of 0.2, then $V = 0.5$).

▶ In the second term, $\left(1-\sqrt{\Delta v}\right)$, Δv is computed by adding 0.5 to the rotation speed of each wheel and taking the absolute value of the difference between them (so if the left wheel rotates at an average of –0.4 and the right wheel at 0.5, then $\Delta v = abs((-0.4 + 0.5) - (0.5 + 0.5)) = abs(0.1 - 1.0) = abs(-0.9) = 0.9)$.

▶ i is the activation of the most active proximity sensor.

Let's pause for a moment to consider the significance of these three components.

Exercise 3.5

Quite a tricky question, but in what way do you think each of these three terms is a measure of the fitness of the robot?

Discussion ....

Floreana and Mondada explain their choice of fitness function as follows:

2.i The term V assesses robots that move at high speed as fitter than slower-moving ones. Note that this is just an absolute measure of speed, so rapid motion backwards, forwards and even in a circle are considered equally fit.

2.ii The term $\left(1-\sqrt{\Delta v}\right)$ favours robots whose wheels move in the same direction. The greater the difference between the rotations of the two wheels, the closer will be the value of Δv to 1, and so the smaller will be the value of $(1 - \Delta v)$. The square root is taken to give strong emphasis to small differences. Robots whose controllers have high fitness in this term will tend to move forwards or backwards in straight lines, rather than in circles.

2.iii The term $(1 - i)$ simply shows how well the robot avoids obstacles. Since i is the highest value of the most active proximity sensor, then the controller which yields the highest value of $(1 - i)$ will be the one that the maintains the robot at the greatest distance from objects.

Note that it would not be possible to maximise all three components together: increasing one would generally be at the expense of others. The evolutionary process has to find a stable balance between the three.

3 *Evolution.* The evolution of controller weights was conducted using the standard GA techniques you met in Unit 1 of this block, including biased roulette wheel selection, biased mutations and one-point crossover, working on a population of eighty genomes. As each generation of controllers was evolved, the weights were passed into a robot situated in the maze and their fitness tested, using the fitness function described above. Testing each generation took about forty minutes.

As one would expect, many of the early controllers were useless, causing the robot to circle endlessly or jam against walls. These were quickly winnowed out by the evolutionary process. But interest focused on the *best* individuals of every generation, and on how well these performed in terms of the three components of the fitness function. Floreano and Mondada made the following observations:

▶ The most successful controllers of early generations – up to about generation 20 – moved in straight lines at low speed, but were not able to avoid obstacles.

▶ Around generation 50 a stable balance between the three terms of the fitness function was found. Once again, a useful way to visualise this is as a space – in this case the three-dimensional space formed by the three terms. The system's trajectory through to the equilibrium zone of the space is depicted in Figure 3.15. At this stage, robots can negotiate the maze and avoid collisions. Further generations of evolution yield controllers that simply increase the speed of the robot.

A special type of laboratory robot known as a Khepera system was used. Khepera robots are connected to a workstation by a fibre-optic cable and their software can run on either the workstation or the robot's internal memory. The transfer of each controller to the robot was thus achieved seamlessly.

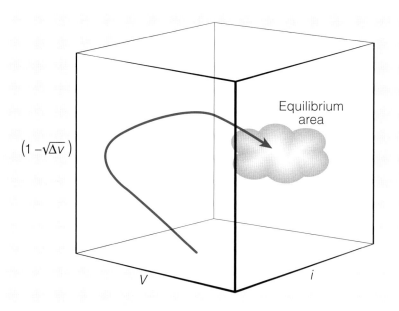

$$\left(1 - \sqrt{\Delta v}\right)$$

Equilibrium area

V

i

Figure 3.15　System trajectory towards equilibrium area

▶ The best robots always moved *forwards*, in the direction indicated on Figure 3.13. But this direction was in no way specified by the fitness function: the Khepera robots, after all, have perfect left–right symmetry, with wheels that could rotate in either direction. The fact that all the controllers evolved forward motion seemed to be an emergent property of the evolutionary process.

SAQ 3.6

Why do you think the robots all evolved forward motion?

ANSWER...

An obvious answer lies in the one asymmetry the robots possessed: the presence of six sensors on one side of the wheels and only two on the other. This would clearly give the robot better sensory resolution in one direction than the other. The evolutionary process automatically selected this direction, although it was not specified directly in the fitness function: a clear example of an emergent phenomenon. However, it was noted that the rear sensors were never inactive. An optimum use of sensor information seemed also to have emerged.

No robot reached anything like the maximum speed of which it was physically capable, even though V was a component of the fitness function. Theoretically, a Khepera robot could move at a maximum speed of 80 mm/s, but the best controllers never moved faster than about 48 mm/s, even after 200 generations or more. This might at first seem like a failure of evolution, but this maximum speed turns out to be another emergent property.

SAQ 3.7

Why do you think the robots stabilised at this maximum speed?

ANSWER...

The answer lies in the rate at which the neural network updated the sensors and motors. The GA found an optimum speed to allow the sensors to refresh the system with new information before making any motor adjustments.

The evolved controllers avoided a problem that affects the simple Braitenberg vehicle illustrated in Figure 3.11. A system with the bare set of feedforward connections depicted there is very susceptible to the kind of deadlock situation shown in Figure 3.16. The problem arises from the symmetry of the connections. If sensors at the same position on either side of the robot are equally activated then their impulses to the motors will effectively cancel one another out, and the robot will become stuck. In the example we're discussing, the recurrent links break the symmetry. The evolutionary process exploited these by finding strongly asymmetric weights for them. Moreover, the speed of the motors at any one time was not just determined by the state of the sensors at that time, as it would have been in a Braitenberg set-up. As with any Elman-style network the recurrent connections helped to preserve a memory of past activity.

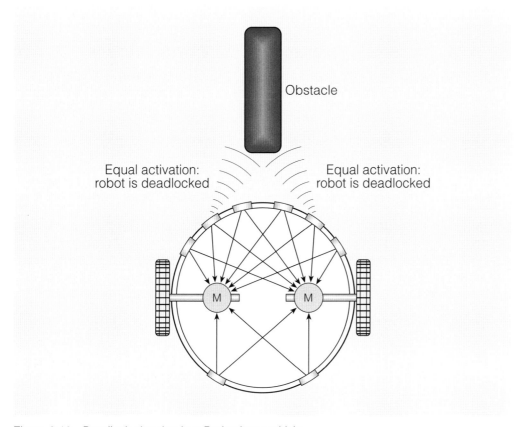

Figure 3.16   Deadlock situation in a Braitenberg vehicle

Floreano and Mondada's work generated a very simple robotic controller, with none of the intricate modularity of Brookes' subsumption architectures. However, all their robot was required to do was negotiate the maze without hitting the sides. We are surely likely to want much more complicated activity from robots than just following a wall. But could truly complex activity really arise in a Braitenberg robot, with sensors wired directly to actuators, and with no internal modules or states? The importance of the recurrent connections in the above case study indicates the need for internal states in even quite simple behaviour. But what use might an evolved robot make of internal modules if it had them?

Case Study 3.3: Evolving modularity

In 1997 Stefano Nolfi published research that began to address this question. He experimented with a series of neural controllers for a garbage-collecting robot. The two-wheeled Khepera robot, which was fitted with a gripper, lived in a rectangular environment bounded by walls, and in which were placed a number of cylindrical objects (see Figure 3.17). The machine's task was to pick up as many of these objects as possible in a given time and dump them on the other side of the walls.

Nolfi points out that the task is, in fact, quite a complex one, involving a sequence of sub-tasks:

1 Move around the environment avoiding the walls.
2 Recognise the objects and move to the correct angle and distance from one to pick it up.
3 Pick up the object.
4 Move to the nearest wall, while avoiding other objects.
5 Recognise the wall and move to the correct angle and distance from one to drop the object over it.
6 Drop the object.
7 Return to step 1.

Moreover, the same sensory state should prompt different actions depending on circumstances. For example, recognising a wall when the gripper is empty should lead to avoidance behaviour; when the gripper is carrying an object, the robot should move to the wall and stop.

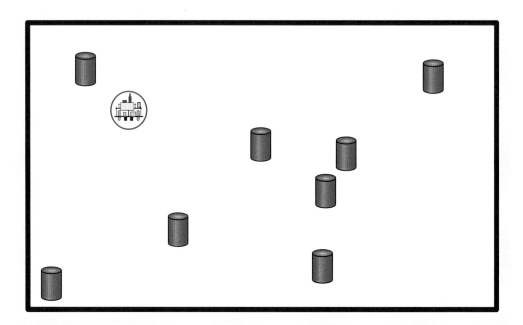

Figure 3.17   Garbage-collecting robot and its environment

The robot was equipped with seven sensors (six proximity sensors and one sensor for the gripper) and four actuators (one for each wheel, one for the pick-up behaviour and one for the drop). The topologies of five different neural controllers, each with seven input units (for the sensors) and four output units (for the actuators), were fixed (see Figures 3.18 and 3.19). Their weights were then evolved and the performances of the five systems compared. In addition to the three conventional homogenous neural controllers illustrated in Figure 3.18(a)–(c), two controllers with a degree of modularity were set up, which I've depicted in Figure 3.19(a) and (b). The first of these (see Figure 3.19(a)) was constructed with a group of four neurons to handle the four actuators whenever the gripper is empty, and a second group of four neurons controlling the actuators when it holds an object. Thus the modular structure of the network was set up to correspond to two distinct sets of distal behaviours.

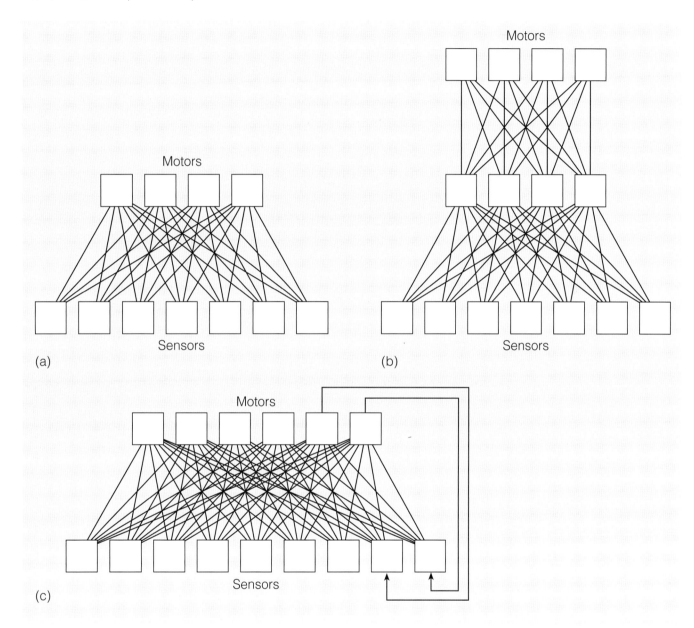

(a)

(b)

(c)

Figure 3.18   Three neural controllers for garbage-collecting robot

Figure 3.19(b) demonstrates a different approach: the controller was designed in such a way that each actuator could be controlled by one or other of *two* modules. Each module consisted of two neurons: one controlled the motor and the other – a *selector* – competed with its counterpart selector in the other module for the right of its module to control the motor. The selector unit with the higher activation would win for its module. Although this structure was pre designed, the way in which the controller actually used the modules was expected to *emerge* from the evolutionary process.

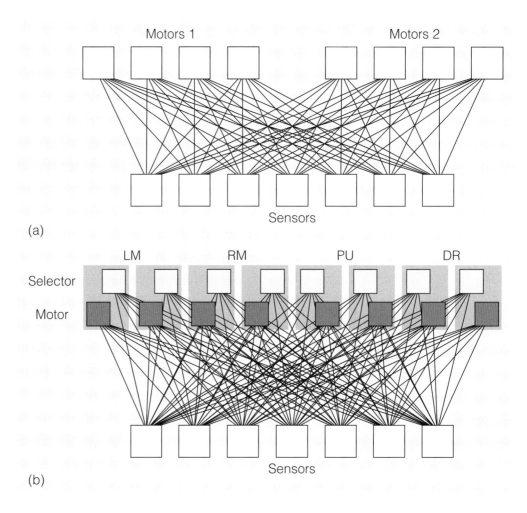

Figure 3.19   Two modular neural controllers for garbage-collecting robot

The weights of all five controllers were evolved using GA techniques, and with the following properties:

▶ The population comprised one hundred genomes.

▶ Each genome was a string of real numbers representing the weights of the network, normalised between −10 and +10.

▶ The fitness function was a combination of the number of objects successfully dropped outside the arena and a measure of the robot's ability to pick up objects.

▶ The best twenty individuals of each generation were selected for the mating pool, each producing five copies of itself, with 4% of its bits randomly mutated; there was no crossover.

▶ Evolution was repeated ten times for each architecture.

Objects were deliberately placed in the path of robots already carrying an object, in order to improve training. After 999 generations of evolution, an analysis of the best controllers for each architecture revealed the following results:

▶ The emergent modular architecture of Figure 3.19(b) was by far the most effective performer: the best individuals in seven out of the ten runs were able to clear the arena with no disasters such as crashing into walls, dropping objects, etc. None of the other architectures came close to this: their best was approximately one or two individuals from the ten runs.

▶ The modular architecture Figure 3.19(a), with internal organisation corresponding directly to two types of distal behaviour, was among the poorest performers.

▶ In controller Figure 3.19(b), the use that the system made of the modules at its disposal was complex, and did not map directly onto distal behaviours. In one of the most successful individuals, the left motor, the pick-up behaviour and the drop behaviour was controlled throughout by only one of the two available modules. The right motor was controlled by complex combinations of *both* available modules, operating at different times. In fact, the majority of the most effective controllers of Figure 3.19(b) tended to divide control of distal behaviours between modules.

Remember a point that I made near the start of this section. Finding the right breakdown of internal modules to produce interesting distal behaviours in a complex and dynamic environment is a hugely difficult and error-prone act of design. The more complex the environment and the required behaviour, the harder a correct decomposition into modules and layers may be to find. Nolfi's experiment above suggests two insights into this problem:

▶ Evolving a controller can free the robot designer from some of the difficulties associated with finding a suitable internal architecture.

▶ Evolution may well arrive at a very effective decomposition in which there is no direct or obvious relation between the proximal interactions within the robot and distal behaviours.

Both of the above case studies involved simple evolutionary techniques, basically the same as those explained in Unit 1 of this block. But evolution is a far from straightforward process, and the details of how it works in nature is by no means fully understood. Let's move on to consider some of the problems of evolutionary theory and then discuss how these might affect evolutionary robotics.

3.3 | Evolution – natural and artificial

A glance around the world should convince anyone that evolution is capable of producing immense success and variety. And the great majority of scientists believe they understand its basic principle: variation under natural selection. But many theoretical details remain to be worked out. This is not the place to review the problems that beset modern evolutionary theory; but there are three theoretical questions especially relevant to the progress of artificial evolutionary computation. Let's briefly look at these now:

▶ *The bootstrap problem.* As you've just learned, evolving controllers for relatively simple robotic activities, such as light following, avoiding obstacles, and so on, works well. However, for more complex activities, artificial evolution using a fitness function based on a simple measure of how well a robot performs the task often fails. The main reason for this is known as the **bootstrap problem**: for a difficult task, small changes in early generations – brought about by crossover or mutation – are extremely unlikely to yield any significant improvement in performance on that task. Performance may well get disastrously worse; and so every new genome might generate very low (or 0) fitness scores. Hence the evolutionary process may never get started.

▶ *Selection vs. adaptation.* In M366, I have made a clear distinction between *adaptation*, a term I've reserved for changes that take place over an individual's lifetime, and which are not passed on to later generations; and *selection*, referring to changes in whole populations over many generations under natural selection. But in the natural world it is clear that both are at work. Indeed, some evolutionary biologists believe that adaptive changes such as learning *are* written back into the genotype of a species by indirect processes – a phenomenon known as the **Baldwin effect**. I won't pursue this idea here, but it is clear that the boundaries between adaptation and selection become blurred in the practice of evolutionary computation. Finding the right balance between them is a particular issue in evolutionary robotics.

▶ *Genotype to phenotype mapping.* Recall that the *genotype* of an organism is the genetic code that governs its development, expressed in the genome inherited from its parents. The *phenotype* refers to the characteristics of the organism itself – body shape, size, colour of eyes, love of chocolate, etc. – as it develops under genetic control. In our case studies above, there was a very clear and obvious mapping between the artificial genotype (the number string) and the phenotype (the set of weights of the neural controller). In nature, the mapping is infinitely more subtle than this. Humans, for instance, have fewer than 40 000 genes to express the extraordinary variety and complexity of the human organism. Clearly the phenotype of every individual is an emergent result of fabulously complicated developmental processes and environmental influences, operating on a relatively simple basic genetic plan. Robotics researchers are only just starting to experiment with complex mappings between genotype and phenotype.

I can now follow up these three points, by examining recent research efforts aimed at tackling the questions that arise from them.

3.4 The bootstrap problem – incremental evolution and co-evolution

I will start with the first of these theoretical difficulties – the bootstrap problem.

SAQ 3.8

Briefly, and in your own words, describe what you think is the *bootstrap problem*, as the term is used in artificial evolutionary systems.

ANSWER..

In artificial evolution, the danger is that all the new variants on an initial population will be of negative or zero fitness, or at best of such low fitness that no improvement is possible and the evolutionary process cannot get started.

This seems especially true in the case of evolving robotic controllers. In a classic optimisation problem, such as finding the maximum of a complex function, or the optimum angles of an aircraft wing, it is quite possible that the fitness landscape will have peaks with smooth gradual ascents towards them. But experiments suggest that for a robotic controller, the fitness landscape is likely to be a huge flat plain, with perhaps only one or two very sharp isolated peaks. An evolutionary algorithm will probably just wander aimlessly around the plain, with no gradual improvement possible.

Two approaches to the bootstrap problem have been adopted in recent research in artificial systems. They are **incremental evolution** and **co-evolution**.

Incremental evolution

In incremental evolution, the evolutionary process is subjected to careful human supervision. In evolving a controller to carry out a complex task, the idea is to start by evolving controllers that can solve a simplified version of the task and then gradually increase the complexity, evolving improved controllers for each new version. There is a short case study illustrating this on the course DVD.

You may feel (as I do) that there is something rather artificial about such an approach. Human intervention – a subjective choice of initial population, manipulation of the environment, carefully planned stages, and so on – is simply not present in a natural setting. An alternative, and more realistic, approach is through the simulation of *co-evolution*.

Co-evolution

Organisms do not evolve in isolation. An evolutionary improvement in one species may create difficulties for another. The development of a more suitably shaped beak in a certain species of finch might mean that they harvest seeds more efficiently, grow in numbers, and so deprive other species of the same resource. Antelopes with longer and more powerful legs will be harder for leopards to catch – a problem for the leopards. Species evolve in a myriad of endless battles with one another. Evolution often seems to be nothing more than a series of arms races.

Many researchers have turned their minds to the question of whether these evolutionary battles can be replicated in the laboratory, and whether **co-evolution** might be an answer to the bootstrap problem. Possibly *two* types of robotic controller, evolving in competition with one another, can chase each other up a ladder of improvement.

Case Study 3.4: Competitive co-evolution

Numerous experiments in artificial co-evolution have been carried out. Among the earliest of these is a classic study by Cliff and Miller (1996) with computer-simulated Braitenberg robots. The idea was to breed two distinct and competing kinds of robot side by side, which they called *pursuers* and *evaders*. The aim of the pursuer was, of course, to catch up with, and bump into, the evader; the aim of the evader was to elude the pursuer.

Each vehicle was governed by a Braitenberg-style neural controller, which generated output signals to the left and right motors. These signals were then used as parameters to an equation of motion that transformed them into an acceleration and a turning angle. Obviously many kinds of system were possible, in which pursuer and evader could have different acceleration and turning capabilities. However, in Cliff and Miller's experiments the capabilities of both pursuer and evader were expressed by the same equation, and so were identical. Both types were also allotted a fixed amount of energy. When this energy supply was exhausted the robot simply came to a stop.

In most of the case studies you've seen so far, the robots have had a neural network controller with a fixed topology, with evolved weights. Cliff and Miller went for a much more complex method of specifying and evolving the sensory-motor and neural architecture of their simulated robots. Here is a simplified description.

The complete structure of each robot was represented by a fixed-length genome along which were a number of genes, each of which expressed:

▶ the position of a neuron within the body of the vehicle. It was possible to encode up to fourteen neurons, but each gene encoding a neuron had a bit which switched it on or off: if this bit was 0, no neuron would appear;

▶ the growth of connections out of the neuron. If a neuron's connections extended beyond the perimeter of the vehicle it became a sensory unit; if it extended into a central zone within the body, it became a motor unit (thus a neuron could be both sensory and motor); if the connections of two neurons met, then they became linked (so some connected neurons could be neither sensory nor motor – these are called **interneurons**);

▶ in neurons that became sensory units, the angle and width of field of the sensor;

▶ whether a neuron was to be duplicated symmetrically on the other side of the vehicle.

I've tried to illustrate some of the features of a neural controller that might be generated by such an encoding in Figure 3.20.

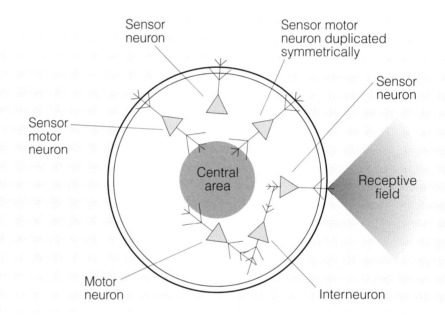

Figure 3.20   Possible neural controller in the Cliff and Miller experiment. All neurons are depicted as triangles with forward and backward projections

New controllers were bred using a fairly conventional GA, with crossover, mutation and rank-based selection, on a population size 100. However, Cliff and Miller were forced to add some refinements. They found this conventional approach was severely affected by the bootstrap problem. Small changes arising from mutation or crossover on a relatively fit controller usually resulted in a drastic drop in performance. So the researchers added **duplication** to the breeding algorithm, a process in which one gene is copied directly onto another area of the genome. It was found that evolution proceeded much more steadily after this modification.

The fitness function used to evaluate individuals of each generation was different for pursuers and evaders. For evaders it was a simple measure of the length of time the individual could avoid being caught by a pursuer. The fitness of pursuers was assessed on a more complex equation comprising a measure of the individual's ability to approach the evader, and its ability to hit it, weighted by the amount of time taken to do so. Many fitness functions were tried before arriving at these.

Controllers were evaluated by a process known as **Last Elite Opponent**, in which the best pursuer of generation n would be matched against the best evader of generation $n - 1$ (and vice versa). Each individual was given fifteen trials and its fitness averaged over these. To make the process more efficient, hopeless offspring, for example ones with no neural connectivity at all, were junked without trial; neurons that had evolved with no connection to others were deleted.

Among many failures, some runs of the algorithm produced successful results. Figures 3.21(a)–(c) illustrate the trajectories of the best pursuers and evaders at Generations 0, 200 and 999, respectively:

▶ At Generation 0, randomly generated, both pursuer and evader have feeble strategies: the pursuer initially moves away from the evader, only later turning back towards it. The evader starts by heading straight for the pursuer and then turns in a circle until it runs out of energy.

▶ After evolving for 200 generations, though, both strategies have improved: the pursuer is pursuing and the evader running away. However, the pursuer travels at such high speed that it quickly runs out of energy.

▶ By Generation 999, each individual has refined its behaviour. The pursuer closely dogs the evader and forces it to use much more energy. However, note that the pursuer still fails to catch the evader.

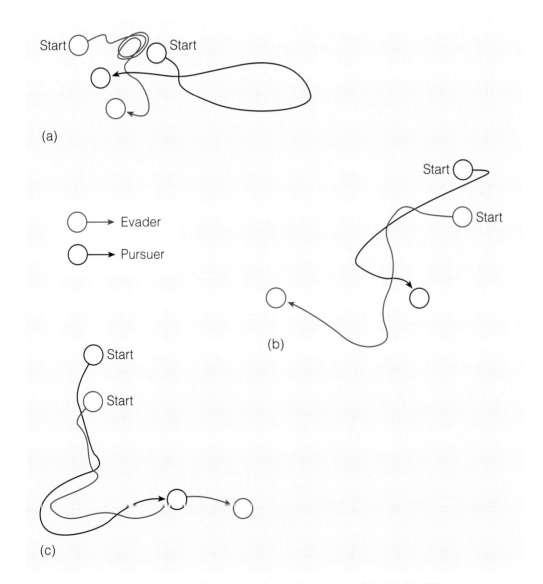

Figure 3.21   Paths of pursuer and evader at Generations: (a) 0, (b) 200, (c) 999

A further interesting result of the experiment was the location of the sensors that both pursuer and evader evolved. The most successful evaders of the final generation tended to have sensors with wide field of view on either side of the vehicle. The successful pursuers had more complex systems but tended to rely mainly on sensors that pointed forward. And this is just what we see in nature: think of the forward-pointing eyes of any predator, such as a cat; or the eyes on the side of the heads of species that are preyed upon (a frog, say).

However, we should not interpret the results of this work too generously. Cliff and Miller themselves end their paper with the reflection that almost all their optimistic assumptions about co-evolution had been busted by the experiment – by its extreme difficulty and the ambiguous nature of the results. One revealing test they applied was to match the elite individual of a late generation against an elite opponent from a much earlier generation. One would expect that an evader from, say, Generation 200 would have no chance against a pursuer from Generation 999. But, in fact, this proved not to be true – just the reverse (see Figure 3.22): the pursuer was *worse* at catching the much earlier evader than it was at catching evaders from Generation 998.

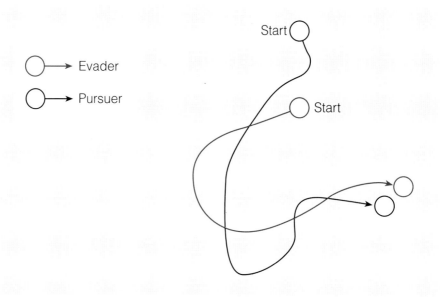

Figure 3.22   Paths of pursuer of generation 999 chasing evader of generation 200

Exercise 3.6

Another rather difficult question, but what do you think might be going on here? Why is the much more evolutionarily advanced pursuer so poor against an opponent from a much earlier era?

Discussion ....

It might be related to the phenomenon known as **cycling**. It works like this: pursuer and evader start with certain strategies (call them P_1 and E_1). Pursuers then evolve a new strategy (P_2) that is better against E_1, so the evader develops a new strategy of its own to cope (E_2). The pursuer then adapts again to strategy P_3, but instead of evolving a new and better strategy, E_3, the evader simply falls back on E_1, which is effective against P_3.

Cliff and Miller's work has been followed up in numerous later experiments, many of them with real robots, with asymmetrical capabilities. The same cycling behaviour has generally been observed. A related issue that later work has revealed is known as the **Red Queen Problem**. Species evolve to cope with their competitors, but at the same time their competitors are evolving too: in fact, everyone is running as hard as they can just to stay in the same place. If we try to picture co-evolution in terms of our conventional fitness landscape, you can see that the presence of multiple competing species makes the whole idea much more complicated. A species may try to move towards higher evolutionary ground, but the movement of other types towards their own fitness peaks constantly *distorts* the landscape for all other species. In fact, the whole landscape concept, so useful in conventional optimisation problems, tends to break down here. The problem all this presents for the designers of co-evolutionary algorithms is that it makes it very difficult to quantify progress and thus to design useful fitness functions.

Researchers have taken a number of different approaches to the cycling and the Red Queen Problems. To consider them any further would take us farther than we need to go. It's sufficient to say that most of the problems with artificial co-evolution remain wide open, and the area is a continuing field of research.

'Well, in OUR country,' said Alice, still panting a little, 'you'd generally get to somewhere else – if you ran very fast for a long time, as we've been doing.'

'A slow sort of country!' said the Queen. 'Now, HERE, you see, it takes all the running YOU can do, to keep in the same place. If you want to get somewhere else, you must run at least twice as fast as that!'

Source: Carroll, Lewis, *Through the Looking Glass*

3.5 Evolution and learning in robotics

Let's start by returning to a key distinction I made in Block 3.

SAQ 3.9

In your own words, distinguish between *adaptation* and *selection*, as used in M366.

ANSWER..

In M366, adaptation refers to the changes that take place over the lifetime of an individual, principally through learning. Selection relates to the evolutionary processes in which whole species alter over many generations.

These seem pretty distinct. We know that Lamarck was wrong: traits acquired during the lifetime of an individual cannot be written into that individual's genes and passed on to the next generation. If I take the trouble to learn calculus, that hardly means that my children will be born with the ability to differentiate. However, I can be fairly sure that the colour of my eyes will be passed on.

But learning and evolution do interact in subtle and indirect ways that are far from completely understood. I've already mentioned the Baldwin effect, where learning may influence evolution. But what about the other way: how does evolution influence learning? To try to get a grip on this question, and how it might have a bearing on artificial evolution, I first need to revisit another distinction I made in Block 3.

SAQ 3.10

In Unit 2 of Block 3, I drew a distinction between altricial and precocial animals. Looking back if you need to, describe in your own words what this distinction is.

ANSWER..

Individuals of precocial species have fully developed capabilities at birth; in altricial species, the young are relatively helpless, and may take a long period of learning to acquire the full capabilities of an adult. An example of a precocial species would be a deer. The clearest example of an altricial species is *Homo sapiens* – ourselves.

How might this distinction relate to artificial evolution? In all the experiments you've looked at so far, the aim has been to produce robotic controllers that are *general purpose* – immediately capable of solving all the problems presented by their environment, without any further change. We might compare these to precocial animals in nature – equipped with all they need from the start. But there are a number of drawbacks to this approach.

Exercise 3.7

Note down what you think might be drawbacks to the strategy of evolving general-purpose controllers.

Discussion ....

I thought of two:

▶ In practice, and for tasks of genuine difficulty, it may be extremely difficult to evolve a controller that is capable of solving from the start *all* the problems it meets. Experiments seem to indicate that in most cases such architectures may not even exist.

▶ General-purpose controllers, if they do exist, are all very well in simple and fixed environments. But realistic environments will be very volatile, changing from moment to moment. It seems almost certain that such a dynamic setting would sooner or later present insoluble problems to a general-purpose controller.

You may have thought of other equally valid objections.

In fact, some form of adaptability must surely be an absolute essential for any agent, natural or artificial, inhabiting a world as unpredictable as our own. Indeed, the whole altricial/precocial distinction may only be one of degree. All but the most simple animals appear to have learning capacities; and even humans have certain inbuilt behaviours. So perhaps our quest in evolving robotic controllers should be to combine adaptation with selection: to aim for systems with certain basic capabilities, which can then be modified and tuned by learning – in other words, controllers with *evolved adaptability*.

Case Study 3.5: Evolving adaptability

Recall Case Study 3.2, where I outlined an experiment in which Floreano and Mondada evolved the weights of a simple neural controller for a maze-following robot. In 1996, these researchers carried out a follow-up to this work, using a different evolutionary approach. In this case, the intention was not to evolve the weights of a controller, but to evolve its *capacity to adapt*.

Using the same maze and two-wheeled robot as you read about in Case Study 3.2, and with the same fitness function and GA algorithm, they worked with a neural controller having the fixed topology that I've illustrated in Figure 3.23. The two motor neurons receive weighted input from each of the eight sensors, as well as from a single hidden unit. The hidden unit has one recurrent connection, giving the controller a total of twenty-seven connections in all.

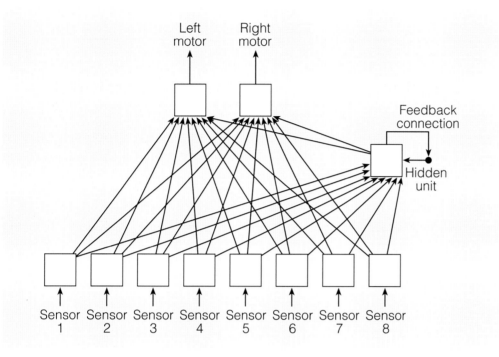

Figure 3.23   Controller for adaptive robot

The properties of each connection were specified by a gene of six bits. In detail, the gene represented the following properties:

▶ The connection could be either *driving* or *modulatory* (one bit – 0 or 1): stimuli on a driving connection were summed in the usual way; modulatory stimuli were also summed and the result used to tune the output of the activation function.

▶ Bit 2 represented whether the connection was *excitatory* or *inhibitory*.

▶ The *learning rule* that the connection would use was specified by bits 3 and 4. Four variations on the Hebb Rule were possible.

▶ The final two bits, 5 and 6, expressed the value of the learning constant η to be used in the learning rule. The four values 0.0, 0.3, 0.7 and 1.0 were allowed.

Note that the weights of these connections were not evolved – only the basic properties of the connection and the way in which the weight could be learned.

After the same evolutionary process as in Case Study 3.2, all the best robots had developed forward movement, as before. Obviously their maze-following ability was not present at 'birth', but emerged rapidly after about two laps of the maze. The researchers noticed a number of stages in the learning process:

▶ Initially robots moved back and forward until encountering a wall. This behaviour seemed quite stereotypical – almost all the robots went through this phase.

▶ The wall-following behaviour was jerky at the start, with the robots trying to turn towards the wall, but rapidly and progressively became smoother.

▶ When they met an angle, the best robots quickly learned to stop, rotate to a new angle and then move forward along the next wall.

But perhaps the most significant result of the experiment was the behaviour of the weights that the robots developed. The conventional neural network view is that weights are learned and then, when they have reached optimum values, become fixed and stable. This was the view of neural network learning that you met throughout Block 4. But when Floreano and Mondada examined the behaviour of the best robots' weights as the vehicle went round the maze, they found that the weights were being adjusted all the time, even after the robots had developed perfect behaviour patterns. Adaptation seemed to be a constant dynamic interaction between controller and environment.

But the evolution of adaptive robots has further surprises in store. Building on earlier work by Todd and Miller, and by Ackley and Litman, the researchers Nolfi and Parisi (1997) conducted significant experiments in this area. Working with simulated Khepera robots, with the usual eight sensors and two motors, they evolved vehicles whose task was to explore a rectangular 60 × 20 cm arena, avoiding collisions with the walls, in search of a target spot on the floor. The target could not be perceived directly by the robot, so the most effective individuals would be the ones that covered the widest area. However, a particular feature of the experiment was that there were two versions of the environment – one with black walls and the other with white walls. The two alternatives required quite different behaviour of the robots in them, because of the nature of their sensors. A black wall would not be detectable until the robot was very close to it, requiring it to move more cautiously than in a white-walled arena, where the walls were detectable from far away.

Two sets of individuals were evolved: *learning individuals*, whose controllers' architecture is illustrated in Figure 3.24; and *non-learning individuals*, with a simplified version. The neural controller of the learning robots was essentially two networks, with some input units – a *teaching network* – and what the researchers called the *standard network*. The standard network controlled the activity of the robot and the teaching network provided feedback to the standard network, causing it to amend weights during learning, using standard backpropagation. The controller of the non-learning robots omitted the teaching network: these individuals had to evolve a strategy that would enable them to perform in either environment without the benefit of adaptation.

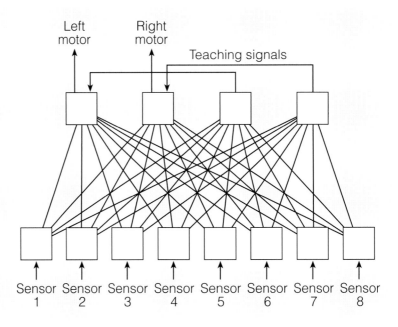

Figure 3.24   Neural controller for Nolfi and Parisi adaptive robot

The weights of both learning and non-learning controllers were evolved using a GA with essentially the same features as in Case Study 3.2, only this time with a 10% mutation rate. The fitness function was simply the length of time it took the robot to discover the target, averaged over ten trials. The fitness of robots of even-numbered generations was tested in the black-walled environment; that of odd-numbered generations in the white-walled. The idea was to produce controllers with the adaptability necessary to learn to live in either environment.

Nolfi and Parisi made a very detailed analysis of the results and drew intriguing – perhaps surprising – conclusions from it. If you have time, you might wish to look at the original paper, but here is a summary of what the experiment revealed:

1   The search strategies of the learning and non-learning robots were compared. Non-learners tended to evolve a workable but rather inefficient approach, keeping well away from walls: a compromise between the most effective strategy for each environment. Learning individuals quickly learned the nature of the world in which they had been 'born' and adopted bolder and more efficient patterns of exploration.

2   The researchers had started with the assumption that learning individuals would – like their non-learning counterparts – evolve a general, compromise solution (embodied in their standard network) which would then be tuned and improved by the teaching network. However, when they compared the performance of learning robots before they had had a chance to adapt with that of non-learning robots they found this assumption was quite wrong. In fact, the performance of (unadapted) learning individuals was much worse than non-learning.

SAQ 3.11

Presumably the weight values of the learning individuals' standard network weights are good for something, having been selected by evolutionary processes. If not for their capacity for coping with the environment, what do you think they might have been selected for?

ANSWER..

One possible answer is that they are selected for their suitability for rapid adaptation. In other words, the weights may have been selected for an inbuilt *predisposition to learn*.

3   In standard neural network training the system is provided with input data. But in robotic learning the learning stimuli presented to the controller depends very much on the activity of the robot *itself*. By rotating, or moving to another part of its environment, a robot can expose itself to new experiences. From a detailed analysis of the sensor readings and the internal behaviour of the two networks, Floreano and Parisi tentatively concluded that the controller had evolved into a state which caused the robot to move in such a way as to expose it to sensor readings that would maximise the differences between the black and the white environment.

Of course, it's possible to argue with Nolfi and Parisi's interpretations. If you refer to the original paper you may wish to do so. However, I don't think that is the point: their results are intriguing and should cause one to think carefully about the nature of learning and adaptability.

It's now time to move on to discuss briefly the last of the issues in evolutionary theory I raised in Section 3.3 – the question of the relation between genotype and phenotype.

3.6 Genotype and phenotype

In all the experiments you've read so far, there has been a simple, clear and direct relation between the structure of the robotic controller being evolved and the genome that is used to represent it. But nothing remotely this straightforward is found in nature. Think of the human genome. It has fewer than 40 000 active genes. There is no conceivable way that the immense complexity of the human body and the infinite variety of human personality could be directly represented in so compact an encoding. As I suggested earlier, a fully grown biological individual – a banana, a fruit fly or a human – must emerge from a set of hugely complex developmental processes and environmental influences operating on a basic genetic specification. How exactly this works in nature is still largely a mystery.

Before I consider the relevance of this to artificial evolutionary systems, you should first remind yourselves of a key biological distinction that has come up a few times already in this block.

SAQ 3.12

In your own words, distinguish between the terms *genotype* and *phenotype*.

ANSWER..

The *genotype* of an organism is the genetic code that governs its development, expressed in the genome inherited from its parents. The *phenotype* refers to the complete set of features of the organism itself.

A major problem, then – in biology as well as in evolutionary computation – is the problem of **phenotype to genotype mapping**, the question of how complex, fully developed individuals arise from a sparse genetic plan. As you've seen, in evolutionary robotics the mapping is usually incredibly straightforward: a single gene (a number, or a group of bits) maps directly to a single feature (a weight, for example). Indeed, this system of representation is so naive that in such circumstances the genotype and the phenotype are essentially the same thing. In such cases, individuals are 'born' as fully developed adults. This hardly ever happens in nature.

There are severe drawbacks to this **direct mapping** approach. An obvious one is that, in order to express more and more sophisticated controllers, the length of the genome has to grow. The size of genotype increases linearly (at best) with the complexity of controller. This in turn makes the search space of the evolutionary algorithms progressively larger, and good solutions increasingly difficult to find. A less obvious drawback is that the direct mapping strategy offers no way of compactly representing *repeating structures*. Some animal bodies are made up of numerous, almost identical segments, stuck together. It would be an incredible waste of resources if each segment had to be expressed independently in its genotypes.

So, the direct mapping approach must have practical limitations in evolutionary computation. What we need is more imaginative ways of genetically specifying controllers, forms of **indirect mapping**, which allow them to develop and adapt under environmental influence. Floreano and Nolfi suggest that the ideal genetic specification will be:

▶ *expressive*: capable of encoding many different characteristics, including the rules that govern the development of the genotype into a phenotype;

▶ *compact*: able to represent the full complexity of the final phenotype in as condensed a form as possible;

▶ *evolvable*: operations such as crossover and mutation should be more likely to produce phenotypes of improved fitness than otherwise.

You can see that in insisting on this last quality, the authors had the bootstrap problem in mind. You've already seen one example of a genotype that specifies a plan for the development of a controller, rather than the controller itself, in Cliff and Miller's work (Case Study 3.4). To illustrate the point further, here is a final case study, in which many of themes of this unit converge.

Case Study 3.6: Evolving evolvability

In an elaborate 1998 study, Jérôme Kodjabachian and Jean-Arkady Meyer evolved neural controllers for simulations of hexapodal walking robots similar to those developed by Beer et al. (see Unit 4 of Block 3). Many of the ideas you've met in this unit – GP, evolutionary algorithms, incremental evolution, recurrent structures and indirect genotype to phenotype mapping – come together in this research. Kodjabachian and Meyer's experiment was a complex one, so again this is a simplified account.

I've illustrated the basic structure of the simulated robot for which controllers were to be evolved in Figure 3.25. Each leg was controlled by four neurons: one sensor and three motor. The sensory neuron was an angle sensor (A), which returned the current angle of the leg. The three motor neurons controlled an upward or downward movement of the leg (UP), the power stroke (PS) and the return stroke (RS). As there are six legs, these neurons are duplicated in six recurring modules.

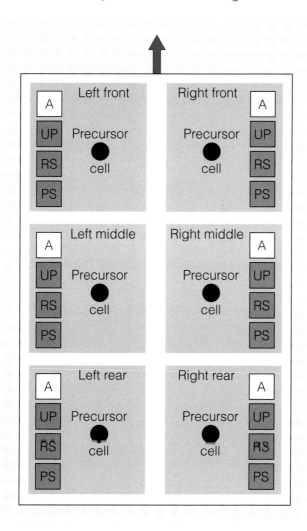

Figure 3.25　Structure of hexapodal robot, with precursor cells in place

Rather than evolve a genotype directly coding a control network, the plan was to evolve a *development program* that would govern the growth of a controller from an initial seed – a *precursor neuron*, one of which was placed in each module. The network would then develop from the precursor cells into a fully fledged controller. The behaviour the controller gave rise to could then be tested on the simulated robot and its fitness assessed (see Figure 3.26).

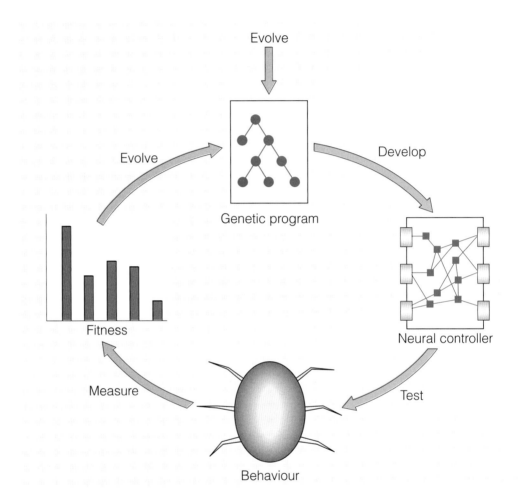

Figure 3.26   Development process for hexapodal robot. The diagram for each stage in the process represents the following: genetic program – a stylised tree; neural controller – a hexapodal robot controller, with leg controllers and an internal network of neurons; behaviour – a stylised six-legged robot; and fitness – a bar chart

Possible programs were expressed as tree structures of the kind you learned about in Section 2.3 above. The terminals of the tree were taken from a set of about fifteen instructions to neurons, controlling their division, growth, activation functions and other properties. Most of the instructions had parameters that were also genetically specified. Figure 3.27 illustrates four execution steps of a simple program acting on a precursor.

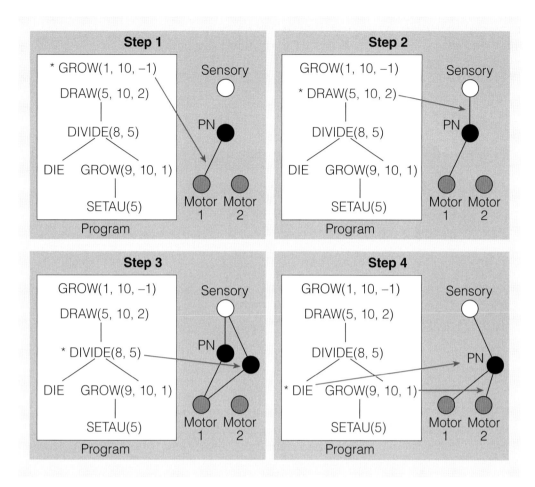

Figure 3.27   Genetic program acting on a precursor cell

Constraints were set on the ways in which the program could develop – limits were placed on the maximum number of nodes and the maximum number of connections each node could form. Other rules were set up to ensure that the program trees were always well formed.

Programs were evolved using the following algorithm:

1   Build a population of randomly generated candidate programs and arrange them in a circle (see Figure 3.28).

2   Select a certain neighbourhood (see Figure 3.28).

3   Randomly select two programs from the neighbourhood and choose the better of these using tournament selection. Then apply three genetic operators to the winner:

   ▶   randomly substitute one of its sub-trees with a sub-tree from another program in the neighbourhood;

   ▶   mutate one of its sub-trees by substituting a randomly generated sub-tree for it;

   ▶   mutate a random number of parameters.

   Each of these has a certain probability of being executed.

4   Assess the fitness of the resulting program.

5   Randomly select two programs from the neighbourhood and choose the worse of these using tournament selection. Substitute the new program for the chosen program.

6   Go back to step 2.

The algorithm terminates after a pre-determined number of programs have been replaced.

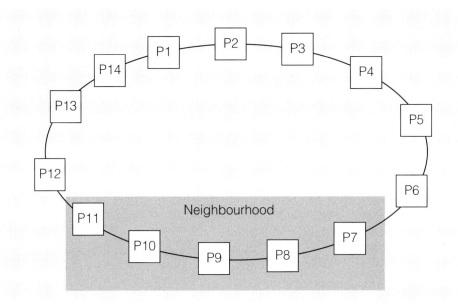

Figure 3.28   Neighbourhood structure for GP selection

As if all this was not elaborate enough, Kodjabachian and Meyer also used a form of incremental evolution. They first evolved controllers for basic movement: these acted directly on the sensory and motor neurons of the robot. The best controller was then fixed as the basic movement controller and a new module evolved to handle the robot's following of a (simulated) pheromone gradient towards its source. This new module interacted directly with neurons of the movement controller. A third module, one that controlled obstacle avoidance, was then evolved to interact with the neurons of the gradient-following module. In this way, the researchers produced a structural design somewhat reminiscent of Brookes' subsumption architectures.

The whole area of genotype to phenotype mapping is clearly one that raises very difficult questions, theoretical and practical. For researchers in the field of evolutionary robotics, these issues are further complicated by the fact that our biological understanding of how the amazing complexity of animal organisms develops under genetic control is still limited. Any further discussion of these questions would take us further than it's possible to go in M366, so now it's time to conclude.

4 Summary of Unit 3

In this unit, I've tried to scratch the surface of two very large and productive areas of current work in AI: GP and evolutionary robotics. I started with GP: the attempt to evolve whole computer programs. I considered how GA techniques could be adapted to such a task, taking in questions of how a program could be represented, how crossover and mutation might work in these circumstances, and some of the practical implications of GP.

Next, I discussed *evolutionary robotics*. Here three major themes of M366 – robotics, evolutionary computation and neural networks – converge in the quest to evolve neural controllers for reactive robots. Through a set of case studies I tried to demonstrate past work in this quest and to raise a number of advanced theoretical questions in artificial evolution – competitive co-evolution, the interaction between evolution and learning, and the mapping of genotype to phenotype – issues which are still problematic today.

As I stated at the start, both GP and evolutionary robotics are active and productive fields of research. Our best hope is that some of you might be inspired to enter one of them yourselves.

For now, though, look back at the learning outcomes for this unit and check these against what you think you can now do. Return to any section of the unit if you feel you need to.

Conclusion to Block 5

Block 5 conclusion

Once again, the problem in writing this block has been to distil the key ideas underlying an immense research effort into a small space.

In Unit 1, I started with a brief, and necessarily superficial, account of the biology of reproduction and evolution, as it is understood today. This led us to discuss how computer scientists have been able to replicate some of these principles in software, in an endeavour known as *evolutionary computation* (EC). I then covered the following concepts associated with EC in the standard *genetic algorithm* (GA):

▶ the representation of potential problem solutions as artificial genomes – bit strings or strings of real numbers;

▶ the fitness function;

▶ the initial genome population;

▶ mutation and crossover;

▶ the biased roulette wheel;

along with some more sophisticated variations on these themes. I then looked at applications of GAs to practical problems in engineering and strategy.

The short Unit 2 dealt briefly with some of the mathematical and statistical theory of GAs. In Unit 3, you saw how the same artificial genetic techniques studied in Unit 1 could be applied to computer programming, so that efficient and correct programs could be generated by an evolutionary process, rather than by conventional programming. In the final section I moved to recent research in robotics, in which GA techniques have been applied to the construction of neural controllers for reactive robots. The discussion threw up some of the problems of contemporary evolutionary theory – natural and artificial – and pointed to future directions of research.

Look back at the learning outcomes for this block and check these against what you think you can now do. Return to any section of the block if you need to.

You will find further case studies, exercises, links and other supplementary material for this block on the course DVD and the course website.

Acknowledgements

Grateful acknowledgement is made to the following sources for permission to reproduce material within this course text.

Figures

Figure 1.2: Department of Clinical Cytogenetics, Addenbrookes Hospital/Science Photo Library.

Cover image

Image used on the cover and elsewhere: Daniel H. Janzen.

Every effort has been made to contact copyright holders. If any have been inadvertently overlooked the publishers will be pleased to make the necessary arrangements at the first opportunity.

References and further reading

Further reading

In writing this text I used many sources. The list that follows is a selection of the sources that I consider you may find helpful in reading further on this topic.

Banzhaf, W., Nordin, P., Keller, R.E. and Francone, F.D. (1998) *Genetic Programming: An introduction*, San Francisco CA, Morgan Kauffman Publishers Inc.

Goldberg, D.E. (1988) *Genetic Algorithms in Search, Optimization and Machine Learning*, Boston MA, Addison-Wesley Longman Publishing Co. Inc.

Nolfi, S. and Floreano, D. (2001) *Evolutionary Robotics*, Cambridge MA, MIT Press.

References

Azaria, Y. and Sipper, M. (2005) 'GP-Gammon: genetically programming backgammon players', *Genetic Programming and Evolvable Machines*, vol. 6, no. 3, pp. 283–300.

Cliff, D. and Miller, G.F. (1995) 'Tracking the red queen: measurements of adaptive progress in co-evolutionary simulations', in Moran, F., Moreano, A., Merelo, J.J. and Chacon, P. (eds) *Advances in Artificial Life: Proceedings of the third European conference on artificial life*, Berlin, Springer-Verlag.

Cliff, D. and Miller, G.F. (1996) 'Co-evolution of pursuit and evasion II: simulation methods and results' in Maes, P., Mataric, M., Meyer J.-A., Pollack, J. and Wilson, S.W. (eds) *From Animals to Animats IV: Proceedings of the fourth international conference on simulation of adaptive behavior*, Cambridge MA, MIT Press.

Floreano, D. and Mondada, F. (1994) 'Automatic creation of an autonomous agent: genetic evolution of a neural network-driven robot', in Cliff, D., Husbands, P., Meyer, J. and Wilson, S.W. (eds) *From Animals to Animats III: Proceedings of the third international conference on simulation of adaptive behavior*, Cambridge MA, MIT Press.

Floreano, D. and Mondada, F. (1996) 'Evolution of plastic neurocontrollers for situated agents', in Maes, P., Mataric, M., Meyer, J.-A., Pollack, J. and Wilson, S.W. (eds) *From Animals to Animats IV: Proceedings of the fourth international conference on simulation of adaptive behavior*, Cambridge MA, MIT Press.

Friedberg, R.M. (1958) 'A learning machine I', *IBM Journal of Research and Development*, vol. 2, no. 1, pp. 2–13.

Friedberg, R.M. (1959) 'A learning machine II', *IBM Journal of Research and Development*, vol. 3, no. 3, pp. 183–191.

Ho, Y.C. and Pepyne, D.L. (2002) 'Simple explanation of the No-Free-Lunch theorem and its implications', *Journal of Optimisation Theory and Applications*, vol. 115, no. 3, pp. 549–570.

Holland, J.H. (1975) *Adaptation in Natural and Artificial Systems*, Ann Arbor, University of Michigan Press.

Kodjabachian, J. and Meyer, J.-A. (1998) 'Evolution and development of neural controllers for locomotion, gradient-following, and obstacle-avoidance in artificial insects', *IEEE Transactions on Neural Networks*, vol. 9, no. 5, pp. 796–812.

Koza, J.R. (1992) *Genetic Programming: On the programming of computers by means of natural selection*, Cambridge MA, MIT Press.

Mitchell, M., Holland, J.H. and Forrest, S. (1994) 'When will a genetic algorithm outperform hill climbing?', in Cowan, J.D., Tesauro, G. and Alspector, J. (eds) *Advances in Neural Information Processing Systems Volume 6*, San Mateo CA, Morgan Kaufmann.

Nolfi, S. (1997) 'Using emergent modularity to develop control systems for mobile robots', *Adaptive Behavior*, vols. 3–4, pp. 343–364.

Nolfi, S. and Parisi, D. (1997) 'Learning to adapt in changing environments in evolving neural networks', *Adaptive Behavior*, vol. 5, pp. 99–105.

Obayashi, S., Sasaki, D., Takeguchi, Y. and Hirose, N. (2000) 'Multiobjective evolutionary computation for supersonic wing-shape optimization', *IEEE Transactions on Evolutionary Computation*, vol. 4, no. 2, pp. 182–187.

Oyama, A. (2000) 'Multidisciplinary optimization of transonic wing design based on evolutionary algorithms coupled with Cfd solver', *Proceedings of the European Congress on Computational Methods in Applied Sciences and Engineering*, Madrid, International Center of Numerical Methods in Engineering (CIMNE).

Reeves, C.R. and Rowe, J.E. (2003) *Genetic Algorithms – Principles and Perspectives: A guide to GA theory*, Boston, Kluwer Academic Publishers.

Index for Block 5